D0913345

THE WELL AND THE SHALLOWS

G. K. Chesterton

THE WELL
AND THE SHALLOWS

IGNATIUS PRESS   SAN FRANCISCO

Cover design and illustration by John Herreid

Reprinted in 2006 by Ignatius Press, San Francisco
Foreword to the New Edition © 2006 by Ignatius Press
All rights reserved
ISBN 978-1-58617-126-1
ISBN 1-58617-126-7
Library of Congress Control Number 2005933382
Printed in the United States of America ♾

CONTENTS

FOREWORD

The Well and the Shallows is one of G. K. Chesterton's last books. But it is not written by a withering, cynical ex-soldier in his dotage recalling past glories on a distant battlefield. Chesterton is still in the thick of battle, still doing what he has always done, and still at the height of his literary power, an incredible feat he maintained for over thirty-five years as a writer. Perhaps the most amazing thing about the consistency of Chesterton's writing is that in the middle of his career, in 1922, Chesterton experienced what he called "the chief event" of his life: he became a Catholic. Why is that so amazing? Because for the most part there is no discernable difference between Chesterton's pre-conversion writings and his post-conversion writings. He defends the same things and attacks the same things and does so with the same skill and ease and paradox and poignancy. Take almost any passage from before 1922 and any from after 1922, and take away any references to particular current events, and any literary critic would be hard-pressed to put a date on it. Why so little difference? Because Chesterton was defending the Catholic Church long before he became a Catholic.

There is, however, one selection of his later writings in which his defense of the Catholic faith takes on a new urgency. A few years after his conversion Chesterton began contributing articles to some Catholic magazines on both sides of the Atlantic, such as *The Universe*, which was published in Ireland, and *America*, the Jesuit journal which was published in, you guessed it, America. The bulk of these essays were reprinted in *The Thing: Why I am a Catholic* (1929) and the present volume, *The Well and the Shallows* (1935). Here, he defends the Catholic faith from all angles, from all attacks, which means writing about anything and everything, which of course is the only thing Chesterton ever writes about—anything and everything. But not only are these essays more specifically Catholic than his other works, there is clearly a sense of foreboding. Hence the urgency.

7

He warns in the introduction that there are not as many jokes in these essays as his readers are used to. He senses before anyone else that there are very dark and desperate days ahead, and that the worst war that the world has ever seen is just over the horizon. The man who some have foolishly accused of anti-Semitism, also saw before anyone else that something terrible was about to happen to the Jews, and he proclaimed that he would die defending the last Jew in Europe.

Chesterton's prophecies are chilling. But what is perhaps more shocking than his prophecies falling on deaf ears at the time, is that everything he said is still true—and still ignored! His warnings are as valid as ever. We seem to have forgotten completely how completely bad the world got and how it got that way. But Chesterton lays it all out in this book. What do these trends have in common: birth control, state-enforced education, scientific officialism, academic deconstruction, and anti-Catholicism? We recognize them as standard elements of the culture in present day America. But they were also the exact same trends seen in the rise of Nazi Germany.

Things will get worse unless we change, unless we repent. That is always the message of the prophet. The prophet wants to be wrong. Too often, however, the prophet is right.

But amid the prophetic warnings, Chesterton still delights. Amid the bold claims boldly argued with a credibility representing a life time of thinking about these things, Chesterton still dances. In spite of warning that there are no jokes, Chesterton still makes us laugh. "The State did not own men so entirely, even when it could send them to the stake, as it sometimes does now where it can send them to the elementary school."

He shines as he takes on relativism:

> It may be incredible that one creed is the truth and the others are relatively false. At the same time, it is not only incredible, but intolerable, to believe that there is no truth in or out of the creeds, and all are equally false. For then nobody can ever set anything right, if everybody is equally wrong.

And Modernism:

> In sum, it is the intellectuals (for want of a more intellectual term) who have suddenly discovered the dangers of a mere novelty, of mere

anarchy, of mere negation. It is because they are so modern that they have rebelled against modernism. It is because they have seen all the new tricks, and played all the new tricks, that they have come to realize that the whole bag of tricks may soon be played out.

There are two particular groups who will probably find this book especially challenging to their ideas, and even better, more likely to read it: Protestants and Catholics.

Chesterton says that he sympathizes with new religious movements. He knows that these people are seeking God. He remembers Christ's dictum that he who seeks finds. But he also notes that most Protestants, whose movements began by protesting against the Catholic Church have lost their original reasons for existing. Instead of becoming Catholic, they simply take on some new form of anti-Catholicism to justify their position of remaining outside of the Church. Protestantism is a large category that has nothing other than anti-Catholicism as its common factor. Chesterton deals with them generally as he considers all the reasons why he would have converted if he had not already done so. He also considers the reasons why the Church is right and everything else is wrong, or perhaps more accurately, why the Church is complete and everything else is incomplete. The Church makes the only complete case not only for defending herself but also for defending everything else that is right and is under attack in the modern world: the family, the poor, self-government, self-control. Protestants who at first feel that their toes are getting stepped on soon realize that Chesterton's complete view of things has their own best interests in mind. The Church is the Well. It is deep and truth is at the bottom of it. Everything else is the Shallows.

It is when Chesterton starts talking about Catholic social teaching that many Catholics start suddenly going deaf or looking for something else to read. Chesterton appeals to the Church's long history of serving the poor and bringing about social justice. He believed that in the modern world these teachings would be best fulfilled in the implementation of an idea known as Distributism, which involves widespread property ownership, self-sufficiency, and family-centered trades. For those who continue to be puzzled by this theory, perhaps the best one-chapter explanation of it anywhere can be found in this book, in the chapter entitled: "Reflections on a Rotten Apple". The surprising claim is that the rise of commercial enterprise has actually done more harm than good in the world, which is an idea that people who have no doubt benefited from capitalism have a hard time grasping. Call it myopia.

Ironically, there are people who enjoy Chesterton's abstract thinking, but get prickly when he goes concrete. It is fine to argue that the Catholic Church is right, and modernism is wrong, but it gets downright uncomfortable when Chesterton starts talking about some of the real practical effects of being Catholic. It may mean making some sacrifices. Giving something up. Suffering, even. But even Catholics must not forget how deep is the Well. Not only do we draw truth from it, we also draw strength.

Chesterton's writing is of that rare quality wherein the whole is present in each of its parts. Each of the essays in this collection somehow epitomizes G. K. Chesterton. And yet there is one that—for me anyway—stands out: the essay on St. Thomas More, the great humanist who died a martyr as he bravely stood up against Henry VIII when that impulsive, power-mad king tried to eliminate the Catholic Church in England. Few people realize that Thomas More was not canonized until 1935. A few years before his canonization, Chesterton said that Thomas More was more important in the present than he was in his own lifetime, and would be even more important in the future. After the canonization, Chesterton wrote the essay that is included here. All of the points that he makes about More—his divine courage, his practical mysticism, his humor, his defense not only of the faith against the state but of the family against the state—are also true of Chesterton himself. The comparison is significant. I believe that Chesterton is more important now than he was in his own lifetime—and he will be even more important in the future.

Dale Ahlquist

INTRODUCTORY NOTE

I was monstrously attracted by a suggestion that these essays should bear the general title of "Joking Apart." It seemed to me a simple and sensible way of saying that the reader of these pages must not look for many jokes, certainly not merely for jokes, because these are controversial essays, covering all subjects on which a controversialist is challenged, and not particular subjects chosen as they are chosen by an essayist. It is an awful revelation of the world of unreason into which we have wandered, that people more practical than I are convinced that if I say that this is apart from joking, everyone will think it is a joke. To my simple mind it seems very much as if I wanted to call a book, "Away from Jericho," and everybody assumed that I had accepted a very general recommendation to go to Jericho. Many essays could be written on this strange modern sensibility to mere verbal allusion, or the introduction of certain words, even to repudiate them. But the only point here involved is that these essays are all under the conditions of controversy, which involve the absolute necessity of disgusting those with whom we disagree on any subject, and boring those who are indifferent to that subject. I have had, if I may say so, a very happy and lucky literary life; and have often felt rather the indulgence than the impatience of critics; and it is in a perfectly amiable spirit that I note that it has involved a certain transition or change. Up to a certain point, I was charitably chaffed for saying what I could not possibly mean; and I was then rather more sharply criticised, when it was discovered that I did really mean it. Now anybody driven to the defence of what he does really mean must cover all the strategic field of the fight, and must fight at many points which he would not have chosen in fancy, but only in relation to fact. He cannot hope to deal only with heresies that amuse him; he must, in common fairness, deal seriously with heresies that bore him. He must settle down to stating his real reasons for contradicting real statements, which are not made by him as statements, and not chosen by him as subjects. All this seems to me, with my mild rationalistic mind, excellently summarised in the words, "Joking Apart."

Anyhow, this is why I have opened this series with an essay called "An Apology for Buffoons," because it is in some sense, I will not say a swan-song (that ornithological metaphor would not occur to me in relation to myself), but at least a sort of summary of my more frivolous mode of writing, and all that I still think may be fairly advanced for it. Unfortunately, a man fighting what he honestly believes to be false can hardly preserve the glorious immunity of a buffoon. He is forced to be serious, and even those who despise him most are driven desperately to take him seriously. But there is one other reason for adding this preliminary note, in connection with the preliminary essay. Since I wrote it, I have come to appreciate much more warmly the admirable work of Mr. T. S. Eliot; and I should like to offer an apology to him for some errors that occurred accidentally in the article itself. It was not he, but another critic, with whom I confused him, who made the particular point against alliteration; and the quotation from him was made from memory; and I have not been able to trace it so as to reproduce the exact order of words. The inaccuracy, if any, does not affect the argument; but the article which I had already planned to put in the same magazine, called "Apology to T. S. Eliot" would have gone far beyond any such verbal point. It would be adding impudence to injury to dedicate a book to an author merely on the claim of having misquoted him; but I should be proud to dedicate this book to T. S. Eliot, and the return of true logic and a luminous tradition to the world.

AN APOLOGY FOR BUFFOONS

There was a time when I appeared in the *Mercury*, covered with blushes, to acknowledge a friendly criticism which asked if my journalism held enough of autobiography; and I attempted with great embarrassment to give thanks for the criticism—and the compliment. My blush has faded; my sense of decency has departed; and I appear now with the shameless purpose of being, not merely autobiographical, but grotesquely egotistical. In a spirit of brazen contradiction, I even propose to be egotistical in disproving the charge of egotism. Nay, in a yet wilder illogicality, I claim to be egotistical in the interests of other people. It is a contradiction in terms; but as the higher mathematics, the higher morality, the higher religion and the rest now entirely consist of contradictions in terms, I go on with a ghastly calm. And I do it because I cannot think of any other way of drawing attention to a real problem of literature, and especially of popular literature (if I may dare to dream of that contradiction also) except this particular line of argument, which inevitably involves the mention of my own case—let us hope along with more amusing ones.

It is commonly alleged of writers that they resent mild criticisms as infamous personal imputations, taking them as seriously as slanders. Without affectation, I fancy my own case to be rather different and even opposite. Most of the adverse criticisms written about me strike me as quite true. Where I am in invincible ignorance, I suppose, is in a proper sense of the importance of the things thus rightly reproved. For instance, a very sympathetic reviewer said that I used too much alliteration; and quoted Mr. T. S. Eliot* as saying that such a style maddened him to the point of unendurance; and a similar criticism of my English was made, I think, by another American writer, Mr. Cuthbert Wright. Now I think, on fair consideration, that it is perfectly truethat I do use a great deal too much alliteration. The only question on which these gentlemen and I would probably differ is a question of degree; a question of the exact

*See apology in Introduction.

importance or necessity of avoiding alliteration. For I do strongly maintain that it is a question of avoiding alliteration—and even that phrase does not avoid it! If an English writer does not avoid it, he is perpetually dragged into it when speaking rapidly or writing a great deal, by the whole trend and current of the English speech; perhaps that is why the Anglo-Saxon poetry even down to Piers Plowman [1] (which I enjoy hugely) was all alliteration. Anyhow, the tendency in popular and unconscious speech is quite obvious, in phrases and proverbs and rhymes and catchwords and a thousand things. Time and tide, wind and water, fire and flood, waste not, want not, bag and baggage, spick and span, black and blue, deaf and dumb, the devil and the deep sea, when the wine is in the wit is out, in for a penny, in for a pound, a pig in a poke, a bee in a bonnet, a bat in a belfry, and so on through a myriad fantastic changes of popular imagery. What elaborate art, what sleepless cunning even, must these more refined writers employ to dodge this rush of coincidences; and run between the drops of this deluge! It must be a terrible strain on the presence of mind to be always ready with a synonym. I can imagine Mr. T. S. Eliot just stopping himself in time, and saying with a refined cough, "Waste not, *require* not." I like to think of Mr. Cuthbert Wright, in some headlong moment of American hustle, still having the self-control to cry, "Time and Fluctuation wait for no man!" I can imagine his delicate accent when speaking of a pig in a receptacle or of bats in the campanile. It is a little difficult perhaps to image the latter critic apparently confining himself to the isolated statement, "Mr. Smith is spick," while his mind hovered in momentary hesitation about how to vary the corresponding truth that Mr. Smith is span. But it is quite easy to conceive an advanced modern artist of this school, looking for some sharp and graphic variation in the old colour scheme of black and blue. Indeed, we might almost invent a sort of colour test, like that which somebody suggested about red grass and green sky as a test of different schools of painting.

[1] "Piers Plowman", an Anglo-Saxon poem attributed to William Langland, expressed in a complex allegory the author's faith in man's need for Christian truth and charity. Although long and irregularly constructed, the poem is considered a magnificent statement of the mind and faith of the late fourteenth century.

We might suggest that Decadents[2] beat people black and yellow, Futurists[3] beat them black and orange, Neo-Victorians beat them black and magenta; but all recoil from the vulgar alliteration of beating them black and blue.

Nor indeed is the reference to these new and varied styles irrelevant. Some of the more bizarre modern methods seem to me to make it rather difficult to have any fixed criticism at all, either of their style or mine. Take, for instance, the case of Mr. T. S. Eliot himself. I recently saw a poem of his praised very highly and doubtless very rightly; though to some extent (it seemed) because it was a poem of profound "disillusionment and melancholy." But the passage specially quoted for commendation ran, if I remember right:

"the smell of steak in passages."

That quotation[4] is enough to indicate the difficulty I mean. For even style of this severe and classic sort is after all to some extent a matter of taste. It is not a subject for these extreme controversial passions. If I were to say that the style of that line maddened me to the point of unendurance, I should be greatly exaggerating its effect on the emotions. I should not like everything to be written in that style; I should not like to wander for ever in passages stuffy with steak (there we go again!) but I cannot think these questions of style are quite so important as these pure stylists suppose. We must be moderate in our reactions; as in that verse specially headed "The Author's Moderation" in the Bab Ballad[5] about Pasha Bailey Ben— another great poem written in a tone of melancholy disillusion.

[2] Decadents were adherents of a French literary movement of the 1880s and 1890s. They rejected moral and religious restraints, emphasized the bizarre and unusual, and exalted sexual aberration. The poet Paul Verlaine was the most prominent figure associated with the group.

[3] Futurism, whose major proponent was the Italian Filippo Marinetti (1876– 1944), was an avant-garde artistic and literary movement that arose just before World War I. It celebrated dynamism, violence and the machine age.

[4] Eliot's quotation is from "Preludes I".

[5] W. S. Gilbert published the "Bab Ballads" in two volumes of humorous verse in 1869 and 1873.

> To say that Bailey oped his eyes
> Would feebly paint his great surprise;
> To say it almost made him die
> Would be to paint it much too high.

I may be allowed to open my eyes for a moment at some of the literary models thus commended to me; but I shall soon close them again in healthful slumber. And when the more refined critic implies that my own manner of writing almost makes him die, I think he over-estimates my power over life and death.

But I have begun with this personal example of alliteration; because a question like that of alliteration is not so simple as it looks; and the answer to it applies to much more important things than my own journalistic habits. Alliteration is an example of a thing much easier to condemn in theory than in practice. There are, of course, many famous examples in which an exaggerated alliteration seems quite wrong. And yet those are exactly the examples which it would be most difficult for anybody to put right. Byron (a splendid example of the sort of writer who does not bother much about avoiding anything) did not hesitate to say of his hero at Quatre Bras that he "rushed into the field and foremost fighting fell."[6] That is so extreme that we might well suppose it described the end of the life and adventures of Peter Piper. But I will trouble anybody to alter one word in the line so as to make it better; or even so as to make it sense. Byron used those words because they were the right words; and you cannot alter them without deliberately choosing the wrong words. This is more often the case in connection with alliteration than many people imagine. I do not mean to claim any such exalted company when I say that, on this particular point of conduct, I agree with Byron. But Byron does not stand alone; Coleridge, a person of some culture, could burst out boisterously and without stopping for breath:[7]

> The fair breeze blew, the white foam flew,
> The furrow followed free.

[6] Byron's quotation is from "The Eve of Waterloo".
[7] The Coleridge quotation is from "The Rime of the Ancient Mariner".

and I do not see that he could have done anything else. I do not think anybody could interfere with that foaming spate of f's, if the verse that followed was really "to follow free."

There is a problem behind all this which is also illustrated in other ways. It is illustrated in the other much controverted question of puns. I know all about the judgments regularly cited as if from dusty law-books in the matter. I know all about the story that Dr. Johnson said, "The man who would make a pun would pick a pocket." How unlucky that the lexicographer and guardian of our language, in the very act of purging himself of puns, should have plunged so shamelessly deep into the mire of alliteration! His example, in that very instance, would alone be enough to prove the first part of my case, even when it is brought forward against the second. Johnson spluttered out all those p's because he was an Englishman with a sense of the spirit and vigour of the English language; and not a timid prig who had to mind his p's and q's by using them in exact alternation with a pattern. But if it came to the old joke of invoking authorities, it would be equally easy to invoke even greater authorities on the side of the pun. Also there is something that is more important to my purpose here. It would not only be easy to quote the puns of the poets; it would be easy to quote the very bad puns of the very good poets. But the question I wish to ask is wider and more essential than all this hotch-potch of snobbery and legalism and A Hundred Familiar Quotations, which goes to make up the modern invocation of authorities. I wish to point out that there is a general attitude of mind, which is defensible; or rather two attitudes of mind, which are both defensible. It is a question of style; but there are here two different styles; because there are two different motives. If one is now criticising the other, I do not merely wish to retort the criticism; but rather to proclaim liberty for both.

It might be roughly suggested thus. It is not merely a question of a man who makes a pun; we might almost ask what is to happen to a man who meets a pun. Is he to cut it dead; is he always to pass by on the other side; is he to disown such disreputable company, as of course our refined stylists would do? I am presupposing that he is not out hunting for puns or similar monsters; I presuppose that he is walking down the street on some legitimate business of his own. But if the grotesque animal actually comes to meet him, if it stands obviously in his path, I think it is natural for him to take it in his stride. At least it is natural to one sort of man engaged in one sort of business; and it is the man and the business that I am here concerned to defend. This is quite a different sort of question from the elaborate construction of such fireworks as a form of art for art's sake; though many men of genius, Hood[8] for example, have occupied themselves even with that. But I am not talking about that. When I was a Pauline, an assistant master received a testimonial on leaving the school for a fellowship at Peterhouse. A solemn upper master made on this occasion the first and last joke of his life by observing in a deep voice, "We are robbing Paul to pay Peter." An old schoolfellow of mine, now a journalist but cynical even at that early age, declared that the older master must have engineered the whole career of the younger, and made him a teacher at that particular school and then a don at that particular College, solely in order to enjoy one moment of supreme triumph in making that single pun. It is not in the sense of such a triumph of engineering that I am here apologising for the pun. I am not speaking of the man whose life's purpose, or even whose purpose, is to make a pun; but of the man who is ready to make puns to serve his purpose. And there is a whole atmosphere and appetite involved here; which we may call if we like the spirit of the demagogue or of the buffoon or of the popular minstrel or of the orator; but which cannot be understood merely in terms of style as style, any more than of art for art's sake.

In any case, things of this sort do exist; coincidences or combinations like alliteration or punning; repetitions or conjunctions that have in prose something of the effect of rhyme in poetry. The only question is how to deal with them when they offer themselves very obviously; as they often do. There are, I think, in a general view, three different ways of dealing with them. First, a man may reject

[8] Thomas Hood (1799–1845) and his son, also named Thomas (1835–1874), were both known for their humorous writings. Chesterton probably means Hood the younger.

them consciously; as the stylist of the serious school of Mr. Wright does when he speaks of "wind and H_2O," or instinctively writes, "In for a penny, in for a Treasury note of the value of twenty shillings." I do not say that these examples are taken from the text; but it is quite a mistake to suppose that such fastidiousness is not a real literary problem. I remember a critic pointing out, even in a master of such direct and telling English as Mr. A. E. Housman, a case in which the poet had obviously written, "The chestnut cast her flambeaux,"[9] simply and solely to avoid writing, "The chestnut cast her candles"—which is twenty times better in every possible way. Second, he can accept them consciously, as I very often do; largely because it is not worth the trouble to reject them. I said a moment ago, "disown disreputable company," because I do not propose to search in a dictionary for an unnatural alternative to "disown". Third, he may accept them unconsciously; and that is a great deal more dangerous than anything else, and a great deal more common than most people imagine. Nobody has yet made an adequate study of the effect of mere phonetics in confusing logic and misleading philosophers. And the worst of that sort of danger is that it is deep and subtle. To decorate an argument with puns and verbal tricks may be a superficial folly. But it is better than the sort of folly that is not superficial.

I am almost certain that many moderns suffer from what may be called the disease of the suppressed pun. I mean that, in men who would disdain to make anything so vulgar as a joke out of a verbal coincidence, there is a subconscious movement of the mind to meet the sound of the word. Thus those who would denounce creeds (a Latin word for anything that anybody believes) are seldom or never, you will notice, moved to describe them by any milder name; they must have a word that sounds like a portmanteau of "crank" and "crabbed" and "greed." They cannot really let themselves go in reviling doctrine. It must be in reviling dogma. They would never sink so low as to make a positive pun about it, as might some poor Popish

[9] Housman's quotation is from *Last Poems* (1922).

buffoon like Erasmus or Crashaw.[10] They would not say of the
Dominicans,[11] "The dogs of God are always dogmatic." But they
are in fact affected all the time by a vague verbal association between
a dogma and a mad dog. It is the accidental sound of the word that
makes them use it so incessantly, and so monotonously, in preference to all other terms, even terms of abuse. On re-reading the end
of Stevenson's not consciously unsympathetic sketch of the Trappists, in the *Travels with a Donkey*,[12] I could swear that he was invol-
untarily influenced by the suggestion that Trappists are caught in a
trap. He cries out, like one who has escaped, that he thanks heaven
he is free to hope, to wander and to love. The logic of it would
suggest that somebody had been trying to capture and imprison him;
a notion which would certainly have surprised the monks very much.
He seems to forget that they also were all free to wander, to love, to
do anything they liked, including going into a monastery; and that
they had gone into the monastery exactly as he had gone into the
mountains. Suppose some burgess of Balham, contemplating the wan-
derer in the Cevennes, had said, "Thank heaven, I am free to dine
properly, sit in an armchair and sleep in a bed." Stevenson might
have replied that he also was free to do these things, but preferred to
do something else. But he never saw the parallel between the journey to the mountain and the journey to the monastery. The terror
of old words and traditional associations choked him like a nursery
nightmare. And I believe he quailed inwardly at the terrible pun of
La Trappe.

Now I for one greatly prefer the sort of frivolity that is thrown to
the surface like froth to the sort of frivolity that festers under the
surface like slime. To pelt an enemy with a foolish pun or so will
never do him any grave injustice; the firework is obviously a firework and not a deadly fire. It may be playing to the gallery; but
even the gallery knows it is only playing. But to associate an enemy

[10] Richard Crashaw (c. 1612–1649) was an English poet and a convert to Catholicism.

[11] This reference to Dominicans is a play on the Latin words *Domini* (the Lord's)
and *canes* (dogs).

[12] *Travels with a Donkey* is Robert Louis Stevenson's account of his trip in 1878
through the Cevennes Mountains of southern France.

always with certain ugly-sounding words, and never with their logical synonyms that sound a little better, is in a very real sense to
poison our own minds. And that is the case with the man who is
subconsciously moved by the sound of words, without realising that
the very assonance is a sort of pun. He must describe a Socialist as
a Bolshevist; because the word Bolshie has a vague savour of Boshy.
He must refer to a Liberal as a Radical, because there is a hard
sound about Rads as there is about Cads. It is a sound heard in
many English names for foreigners, from the time that we first talked
about Rapparees[13] to the time when we began, more faintly, to talk
about Yankees. The criticism of these foreigners is not in question;
but the point is this. If a man can say about a Yankee what he would
hardly say about an American, or even about a Northern American,
then he is allowing this shadow of a pun, or sound of a word, to
spoil his sense of justice and reality. He is obscurely confusing the
word Yank with the word Swank. If he can speak of a Froggy more
scornfully than he could really speak of a Frenchman, then he is
being verbally affected by the word frog, as was the other man by
the word dog. I do not think it matters how much we play about
with these puns or rhymes or resemblances, or echoes of sound, so
long as we are obviously doing it on the surface for the sake of the
sound. Exactly when this sort of style becomes dangerous to the
sense is when it is concealed, as these more sensitive stylists would
conceal it. It is so that class-consciousness is worse than ever when
it is class subconsciousness. It is so that the professed impartiality of
certain academic historians stinks with their buried prejudice.

Compared with this, I do think there is something sporting about
conscious buffoonery. As it is embarrassing to use the egotistic example, I will take the example of a very much more distinguished person, who is in this respect of the same type or temper as I; I mean
Mr. Bernard Shaw. There used to be at one time a great fashion of
arguing about Shaw and Shakespeare, and, by the way, that must
surely have been an artificial trick of alliteration. Yet it would be
dangerous to suggest to Shaw that he copied Shakespeare, and there

---

[13] Rapparees were Irish freebooters of the seventeenth century.

are difficulties even in telling Shakespeare he copied Shaw. Anyhow, one of the few things in which there is a real resemblance between Shaw and Shakespeare is this; that they both seem so very often to make jokes that are not worth making. When Polonius says he was Julius Caesar; whom Brutus killed in the Capitol; and Hamlet is made to answer, "It was a brute part of him, to kill so capital a calf there," I do not imagine that Shakespeare, any more than anybody else, thought that the two puns were the most perfect and pointed specimens of wit. But he did think it vital to the story that Hamlet should make a flippant remark of some sort at that moment; and he thought it a very probable sort of flippant remark for him to make. There are any number of flippancies in Shaw's plays that are no better than this, and serve no other purpose than this. But the point is that flippancies of this sort are only used by a very serious person; and Mr. Bernard Shaw is a very serious person. He wants to say something. He has something to say. If ever the perfect stylistic critics should find themselves in such a peculiar position, they will discover the nature of these temptations to flippancy.

It is not an idle contradiction to say that Mr. Shaw is flippant because he is serious. A man like Mr. Shaw has the deliberate intention of getting people to listen to what he has to say; and therefore he must be amusing. A man who is only amusing himself need not be amusing. Generally, when he is a perfect and polished stylist, he is not. And there is a good deal of misunderstanding about the relative moral attitude of the two types; especially in connection with the old morality of modesty. Most persons, listening to these loud flippancies, would say that Mr. Bernard Shaw is egotistical. Mr. Bernard Shaw himself would emphatically and violently assert that he is egotistical; and I should emphatically and violently assert that he is not. It is not the first time we have somewhat tartly disagreed. And perhaps I could not more effectively perform the just and necessary public duty of annoying Mr. Shaw than by saying (as I do say) that in this matter he really inherits an unconscious tradition of Christian humility. The preaching friar puts his sermon into popular language, the missionary fills his sermon with anecdotes and even jokes, because he is thinking of his mission and not of himself. It does not matter that Mr. Shaw's sentences so often begin with the pronoun "I." The Apostles' Creed begins with the pronoun "I"; but it goes on to rather more important nouns and names.

Father Ronald Knox,[14] in his satire on Modernism, has described the courteous vagueness of the Oxford manner which

> ... tempering pious zeal
> Corrected, "I believe" to "One does feel."

And though I have much of such courtesy to be thankful for, both in conversation and criticism, I must do justice to the more dogmatic type, where I feel it to be right. And I will say firmly that it is the author who says, "One does feel," who is really an egoist; and the author who says, "I believe," who is not an egoist. We all know what is meant by a truly beautiful essay; and how it is generally written in the light or delicate tone of, "One does feel." I am perfectly well aware that all my articles are articles, and that none of my articles are essays. An essay is often written in a really graceful and exquisitely balanced style, which I doubt if I could imitate, though I might try. Anyhow, it generally deals with experiences of a certain unprovocative sort in a certain unattached fashion; it begins with something like ...

> "The pond in my garden shows, under the change of morning, an apprehension of the moving air, hardly to be called a wave; and so little clouding its lucidity as to seem rather vacuity in motion. Here at least is nothing to stain the bright negation of water; none of those suburban gold-fish that look like carrots and do but nose after their tails in a circle of frustration, to give some sulky gardener cause to cry 'stinking fish'. The mind is altogether carried away upon the faint curve of wind over water; the movement is something less solid than anything that we can call liquid; the smoke of my light Virginian cigarette does not mount more unsubstantially towards the sky. Nor

[14] Monsignor Ronald Knox (1888–1957) was one of the most famous Anglican converts to Catholicism in twentieth-century England. He served as Catholic chaplain at Oxford University from 1926 to 1939, produced a fresh translation of the Vulgate Bible, authored detective stories and became one of England's most articulate Catholic apologists.

indeed inaptly: it needs some such haven of patriarchal mildness to accent sharply the tang of mild tobacco; alone perhaps, of all the attributes of Raleigh's red-haired mistress, rightly to be called virginal."

I think I might learn to do it some day; though not by a commercial correspondence course; but the truth is that I am very much occupied. I confess to thinking that the things which occupy me are more important; but I am disposed to deny that the thing I think important is myself. And in justice not only to myself but to Mr. Shaw and Mr. Belloc and Mr. Mencken and many another man in the same line of business, I am moved to protest that the other literary method, the method of, "One does feel," is much more really arrogant than ours. The man in Mr. Shaw's play remarks that who says artist says duellist. Perhaps, nevertheless, Mr. Shaw is too much of a duellist to be quite an artist. But anyhow, I will affirm, on the same model that who says essayist says egoist. I am sorry if it is an alliteration, almost a rhyme and something approaching to a pun. Like a great many such things, it is also a fact.

Even in the fancy example I have given, and in a hundred far better and more beautiful extracts from the real essayists, the point could be shown. If I go out of my way to tell the reader that I smoke Virginian cigarettes, it can only be because I assume the reader to be interested in me. Nobody can be interested in Virginian cigarettes. But if I shout at the reader that I believe in the Virginian cause in the American Civil War, as does the author of *The American Heresy*,[15] if I thunder as he does that all America is now a ruin and an anarchy because in that great battle the good cause went down—then I am not an egoist. I am only a dogmatist; which seems to be much more generally disliked. The fact that I believe in God may be, in all modesty, of some human interest; because any man believing in God may affect any other man believing in God. But the fact that I do not believe in gold-fish, as ornaments in a garden pond, cannot be of the slightest interest to anybody on earth, unless I assume that some people are interested in anything whatever that is connected

[15] Chesterton is referring to Christopher Hollis (1902–1977), English author, Conservative politician and convert to Catholicism.

with me. And that is exactly what the true elegant essayist does assume. I do not say he is wrong; I do not deny that he also in another way represents humanity and uses a sort of artistic fiction or symbol in order to do so. I only say that, if it comes to a quarrel about being conceited, he is far the more conceited of the two. The one sort of man deals with big things noisily and the other with small things quietly. But there is much more of the note of superiority in the man who always treats of things smaller than himself than the man who always treats of things greater than himself. The latter at least must be very small if he does not feel that they are greater.

Now the next two steps bring us to the climax of the matter. First, this dogmatist is always something of a demagogue. Second, this demagogue is always something of a buffoon. I am very far from denying that he becomes too much of a demagogue and too much of a buffoon. But he does not do so because he prefers superficial things, but rather because he is concerned with fundamental things. If I may illustrate my meaning by one of those deplorable verbalisms over which we are all lamenting, I would say that it is exactly because he is concerned with fundamentals that he is tempted to tickle the groundlings. He is interested in primary facts; and one of those primary facts is the people. He may make jokes and play to the gallery; but there is something more than a joke for him in the phrase which calls the gallery the gods.

I also am a tub-thumper; and I exaggerated my meaning a moment ago, in the necessity of defending myself, of defending Mr. Shaw and (most exciting of all) of defending Mr. Shaw against Mr. Shaw. I do not really mean, of course, that the essayist is an egoist in any selfish sense. Nobody in the world, I imagine, gets more good than I do out of good essays like those of Mr. Max Beerbohm or Mr. E. V. Lucas or Mr. Robert Lynd.[16] I only ask, in all seriousness, that

---

[16] Max Beerbohm (1872–1956) was an English satirist and caricaturist. Edward Verrall Lucas (1868–1938) was an English essayist and biographer of Charles Lamb. Robert Lynd (1879–1949) was an English journalist best known for his essays that appeared regularly in the *New Statesman* from 1913 to 1945.

they should understand the necessities of our sort of self-assertion as well as recognising the existence of their own. And I do ask them to believe that when we try to make our sermons and speeches more or less amusing, it is for the very simple and even modest reason that we do not see why the audience should listen unless it is more or less amused. Our mode of speech is conditioned by the fact that it really is what some have fancifully supposed the function of speech to be; something addressed by somebody to somebody else. It has of necessity all the vices and vulgarities attaching to a speech that really is a speech and not a soliloquy.

I have come to the conclusion that this last point is too plain to be understood. Some of the simplest things of human history are now quite invisible to minds that have grown accustomed to sub-division or specialism. Thus the idea of the vow, one of the first facts about our social foundation, is not disputed or denied; it is simply nibbled out of existence by people who do not know that it exists. It is so with the gesture of the sacrifice, without which man is hardly human; and it is so with the gesture of the speaker or the singer dealing directly with the people. I found a case of this con-fusion in connection with this point, after I had tried to suggest it in an article in the *Mercury* called, "The True Case Against Cliques." A critic in the American *Bookman* immediately assumed that it was only the old and conventional case against cliques. He got it into his head that I had merely been grumbling about log-rolling; and he said that Aristophanes and Euripides had their cliques and backers like anybody else. It seems to me that American criticism, so far from being merely crude, is rather too traditional. It has a curious conservative way with it and labels things in the manner of a museum; indeed I found in the same number a very Victorian article called, "Science and Religion," in which these two forces were studied under the representative figures of Charles Darwin and Mr. Moody.[17] Many things have been written about Science and Religion; but I should not feel myself overwhelmed by the onward rush of a new world which had never considered any science later than Darwin or

[17] Dwight L. Moody (1837–1899) was an American revivalist.

any religion better than Moody and Sankey.[18] Many things have also been written against log-rolling and literary clannishness; but I did not write anything against them or indeed anything about them. What I was trying, I fear rather clumsily, to express was that there is now an entirely new danger in the clique; because it is not merely a clique. It has taken on the character of an interpreter; by hypothesis the interpreter of something unintelligible; and its existence encourages the artist to be unintelligible, when it is his whole function to be intelligible. The artist is the man who is more and not less intelligible than other men; it is the mass of men whose feelings remain relatively incomprehensible, even to themselves.

Aristophanes undoubtedly had his faction and in that sense his clique. But I gravely doubt whether his audience needed anybody to explain to them that when the dead man said, "May I come to life if I do," it was a joke and a parody of the phrase, "May I die if I do." In other words, the jokes of Aristophanes, like the jokes of Bernard Shaw, were good jokes; but they were obvious jokes. There was not normally any question of a new and secretive sense of humour, which only a certain school of aesthetes or critics could understand. The buffoonery of Bernard Shaw is in this respect like the buffoonery of Aristophanes; or if it be difficult to make sure of the conditions in the time of Aristophanes, the element of obviousness is equally obvious in the best jokes of Molière or the best jokes of Dickens. The whole case for buffoons is that jokes ought to be obvious. We may even say that they are not really jokes unless they are obvious. There are, of course, special conditions for the thing called irony; in which it is the joke that somebody does not see the joke. But even there that person is not the audience; or if he is, the irony has failed. But in any case there is here a joke that the critics cannot apparently see; and a joke which is also something of a tragedy. There is under the surface of all this conspiratorial culture, a fantastic notion of new and even disparate psychologies breaking up the brotherhood of the common human mind; incommunicable or at least without communication between one another. As Mr. Wells imagined

---

[18] Ira D. Sankey (1840–1908) was a hymn writer and Dwight Moody's music director.

man evolving into two animals, we are really called on to imagine mind breaking up not so much into cliques as into species. The buffoon may make bad jokes; I myself, who am a very minor buffoon to be mentioned with Mr. Shaw, let alone Aristophanes, do regularly and as a matter of business make a multitude of bad jokes. I do it for reasons connected with the duties of demagogy, and I am not defending it here, but rather something much more important. Buffoons may make bad jokes; but it is quite another thing that a man should make a joke and another man *really* not know that it is a joke at all. The first man may think it a good joke and the second a bad joke; that is normal and has always been; in the case above-mentioned my critic and I can embrace in agreeing that it is a bad joke. But if aberration and mystery be so deliberately cultivated that the jest of one school is not a jest at all but only a riddle to another, we are at the beginning of a schism more perilous than any in the past. We are suffering Taste to tear men asunder as they have never been torn asunder by religion or revolution or the wars of the world. In other times there were other and nobler examples of this direct relation between the maker and mankind. The orator could make a mob feel like an army of heroes; the prophet or preacher could isolate every soul in a crowd and make each feel immortal. To make what is now called a popular speech it is indeed necessary to make it only too like what is called an after-dinner speech; to keep our connection with the normal life only by a thin thread of flippancy. But at least the connection is kept; and something remains of what is really the archetypal relation implied in the very existence of the arts. It is not altogether our fault if a chasm has opened in the community of beliefs and social traditions, which can only be spanned by the far halloo of the buffoon.

MY SIX CONVERSIONS

I. The Religion of Fossils

At least six times during the last few years, I have found myself in a situation in which I should certainly have become a Catholic, if I had not been restrained from that rash step by the fortunate accident that I was one already. The point is not merely personal but has some representative interest, because our critics constantly expect the convert to suffer some sort of reaction, ending in disappointment and perhaps desertion. As a rule, the most that they will concede to us is that we have found peace by the surrender of reason; which generally means in practice that we pass the rest of our lives in interminable controversies with a perpetual appeal to logic. But, as a fact, it is in a rather peculiar sense, the other way about. The strongest sort of confirmation often comes to the convert after he has received enough to establish conviction. In these articles I propose to discuss some examples of this singular sort of post-conversion conversion. I mean that things have happened, since I was received into the Church, which would in any case have rendered impossible any intellectual position outside the Church, and especially the position in which I originally found myself. One occasion was the Parliamentary settlement of the controversy on the Prayer-Book—or Prayer-Books.[19] Another was the Lambeth decision, or indecision, about Birth-Control. But I will take first the example of the latest turn of political events in Europe. I take it first because it is both typical and topical; that is, it gives perhaps the clearest and simplest example of the sort of thing I mean, and it is a thing of which the facts are fresh and familiar to everybody, even those who live only from day to day with the assistance of the daily Press; that very synthetic substitute for daily bread. But in order to explain what I think has really happened, rather more lucidly than the daily Press explains it, it is necessary to say a preliminary word about the Protestant

[19] Chesterton is referring to the controversy surrounding the revised *Book of Common Prayer* of 1928.

Reformation and the sense in which its consequences, rather than itself, continue to bewilder and mislead Christendom.

Men of the type or school of Bishop Barnes or Dean Inge[20] are, as we know, very fond of appealing to the discoveries of science; generally the not very recent discoveries of nineteenth-century science. They delight in dealing with what my grandfather would have called the Testimony of the Rocks; the geological record of natural development; and they often treat fossils and similar traces as if they were sacred hieroglyphics, by which some priesthood had symbolised the secret of the universe. And yet it is doubtful, it is more than doubtful, whether one of the Broad Church ecclesiastics would be soothed and flattered if I addressed him personally as an Old Fossil. Nor indeed should I dream of indulging in this playful form of social address; since there are truths, or half-truths, that cannot be coarsely stated without giving rise to misunderstanding even about their true meaning.

In one sense these liberal theologians are interested in fossils. They continue to demonstrate the Darwinian theory from the geological record, by means of all the fossils that ought to be found in it. They will even explain luminously why the geological evidence does not apparently exist; and they seem to think that this is quite as convincing as if it did exist. But I doubt whether they have really thought profoundly and delicately about what a fossil is, or there would be no danger of their resenting so innocent and inoffensive a comparison. For a fossil is really a very curious thing. A fossil is not a dead animal, or a decayed organism, or in essence even an antiquated object. The whole point of a fossil is that it is the *form* of an animal or organism, from which all its own animal or organic substance has entirely disappeared; but which has kept its shape, because it has been filled up by some totally different substance by some process of distillation or secretion, so that we might almost say, as in the medieval metaphysics, that its substance has vanished and only its

---

[20] Ernest William Barnes (1874–1953) was an Anglican bishop of Birmingham; William Inge (1860–1954) was dean of St. Paul's Anglican cathedral, London, from 1911 to 1934.

accidents remain. And that is perhaps the very nearest figure of speech we can find for the truth about the New Religions, which were started only three or four hundred years ago. They are Fossils.

It is easy to see the sense in which they are now dying. But in a much deeper sense, they have long been dead. The extraordinary thing about them was that they really died almost as soon as they were born. And this was due to a fact not always emphasised, but which always strikes me as the most outstanding fact of the mysterious business; the incredible clumsiness of the Reformers. The real Protestant theologians were such very bad theologians. They had an amazing opportunity; the old Church had been swept out of their way, along with many things that were really unpopular, and some things that were deservedly unpopular. One would suppose it was easy enough to set up something that would at least look a little more popular. When they tried to do it, they made every mistake that they could make. They waged an insane war against everything in the old faith that is most normal and sympathetic to human nature; such as prayers for the dead or the gracious image of a Mother of Men. They hardened and fixed themselves upon fads which anybody could see would pass like fashions. Luther lashed himself into a sort of general fury, which obviously could not last; Calvin was logical, but used his logic for a scheme which humanity manifestly would not long find endurable. Perhaps the most successful were those who really had no ideas to offer at all; like the founders of the Anglican Church. They at least did not exasperate human nature; but even they showed the same blindness, in binding themselves instantly to the Divine Right of Kings, which was almost immediately to break down.

For this reason, there is really no historical doubt about what Protestantism did; it died. It did not die because the Protestants were wrong; Mahomet, for instance, was a far shrewder person, and his heresy has not died. The creed of the Protestants died, not because they were wrong, but because they were wrong-headed. They did not really think what they were doing; and this was chiefly because the real driving force behind them was the impatient insolence and avarice of new nobles and rebellious princes. But, anyhow, the theological and theoretical part of their work withered with extraordinary rapidity; and the void that was left was almost as rapidly filled with other things. What those things were is clear enough in many cases, including cases much more apparently harmless; but it is clearest of all in what is confronting us to-day; the Race Religion of the Germans.

Needless to say, there was no such nonsense talked in Luther's time, or for long after his time; and, least of all, to do him justice, by Luther. Germans were turbulent and a little barbaric, as he was himself; but it is only fair to him to say that he was a Christian, in the sense that he believed that nothing could be done except in the strength of Christ. A superbly typical story reaches me from Germany; that some of the Nazis started out to sing the great reformers's famous hymn, "A strong fortress is our God" (which sounds quite promisingly militaristic), but found themselves unable to articulate the very words at the beginning of the next verse, which ran, "Of ourselves we can do nothing." Luther did, in his own mad way, believe in humility; but modern Germany believes simply, solely and entirely in pride. That is an example of what I mean by a void being filled up, not only by another substance, but actually by an antagonistic substance.

Luther was subject to irrational convulsions of rage, in one of which he tore out the Epistle of St. James from the Bible, because St. James exalts the importance of good works. But I shudder to imagine into what sort of epileptic convulsion he would have fallen if anybody had told him to tear out the Epistles of St. Paul, because St. Paul was not an Aryan. Luther, if possible, rather exaggerated the weakness of humanity, but at least it was the weakness of all humanity. John Knox achieved that queer Puritan paradox, of combining the same concentrated invocation of Christ with an inhuman horror and loathing for all the signs and forms and traditions generally characteristic of Christians. He combined, in the way that puzzles us so much, the adoration of the Cross with the abomination of the Crucifix. But at least John Knox would have exploded like dynamite, if anybody had asked him to adore the Swastika. All this new Nordic nonsense would seem to have nothing whatever to do with Protestant theology; or rather to be completely contrary to it. No one is more sincerely glad than we are to know that some of the German Protestants are still most consistent and courageous Christians; and that a definite number of the Lutherans still have some sort of remote connection with Luther. But, taking the development simply as an historical development, as a part of the science and philosophy of history, it is obvious by this time that the hollow places that were once filled with the foaming fanaticism of the first Reformation doctrines are now filled with a foaming fanaticism of a totally different kind. Those who are rebelling like Luther are rebelling against Luther.

The main moral of this is so large and simple and striking, that it will soon be impossible to conceal it from the world. It is the simple fact that the moment men began to contradict the Church with their own private judgment, everything they did was incredibly ill-judged; that those who broke away from the Church's basis almost immediately broke down on their own basis; that those who tried to stand apart from Authority could not in fact stand at all. Islam stood by being stagnant; it is not unfair to say it stood up by lying down. But Protestantism could not stand in the staggering rush of the West; it could only maintain itself by ceasing to be itself, and announcing its readiness to turn into anything else.

II. When the World Turned Back

For the first forty years of my life, practically no man in the world, and certainly no man of the world, had any doubt whatever about what Matthew Arnold called, "the way the world is going." A man did not necessarily agree with Matthew Arnold, who seemed to think that he must necessarily go the way the world was going. Some regretted ages that were gone; some again were prepared to go farther than others, some to go faster than others; some almost passionately desired to go slow. But all agreed that it was, in the vulgar phrase, going it; and still going strong. It was, very broadly, the demand for freedom and fraternity flowing from the French Revolution and the American Revolution, making towards an ideal of democracy.

Elements were indeed mixed in it, which logically had very little to do with each other. There was a tendency to materialism, to monism or to scepticism, which I rejected long before I was a Catholic. There was an element of equal justice, and the dignity of all citizens, which I accepted long after I was a Catholic; and which I accept still. But I assumed, like everybody else, that the main movement was still moving; and would presumably go on moving. There were three ways in which it could be recognised by a Catholic, or a man of increasingly Catholic sympathies. (1) He could say that this was the way the world was going; and so much the worse for the world. He could say the world would certainly go further and fare worse. (2) He could say, with considerable truth, that no such movement that was purely secular really touched the question that was purely spiritual. To take a simple example, the most ideal Republicans could not somehow get out of the human habit of dying; and generally of wondering whether dying meant being completely dead. Democracy could not satisfy all desires, even if it could purge itself enough to satisfy all democratic desires. (3) He could look forward, with some historical justification, to a time when any temporal quarrel between the Church and the Republic should end in a real and reasonable reconciliation of the truths in both; as St. Thomas reconciled the philosophy of Aristotle with the religion of Augustine. Something like this has largely been done, in recent Papal pronouncements; but the point is here that whether or no the Church could close this particular quarrel with the world, every one was certain that a quarrel with democracy *was* a quarrel with the world. In short, a Catholic might reject the present progress; or say his creed was independent of the present progress; or say his creed would find a place for the present progress. But everybody believed that the progress of the present would be the progress of the future.

Then came the astounding judgments; the strange signs of Apocalypse. First the Great War; then the paradox of Fascism in Italy; then the parody of Fascism in Germany. Now these things have left in the minds of all thinking men (as the Rationalist Press Association would say) an enormous overturn or reversal of thought, which has nothing whatever to do with thinking any of these movements

right or wrong. It is very vital to realise that the change is something more fundamental than agreement or disagreement with the
factions concerned. A man may think the war waged by the Allies
justifiable, as I did and do; he may think that the stroke of Mussolini
had considerable justification, or even that the stroke of Hitler achieved
many things that were just. Or he may think exactly the opposite,
and regard the whole militant epoch as a relapse into blood and
barbarism, from the first recruit of Kitchener's Army[21] to the last
ruffian dripping with the blood of Dollfuss.[22] But there is a changed
landscape at the back of all these fighting figures; and it is a landscape like an earthquake. What a man knows, now, is that the whole
march of mankind can turn and tramp backwards in its tracks; that
progress can start progressing, or feeling as if it were progressing, in
precisely the contrary course from that which has been called progress
for centuries. It can not only lose but fling away all that its fathers
fought for and valued most; it can not only restore but restore exclu-
sively all that its grandfathers were forced to abandon, or felt themselves unable to defend. The whole world is moving again; but it is
moving the other way.

To-day *this* is the way the world is going, if there is any such
thing. But in fact there is no such thing. A Catholic perhaps should
have seen it from the first; but many a Catholic has only seen it in
a flash at the last. There is no way the world is going. There never
was. The world is not going anywhere, in the sense of the old opti-
mist progressives, or even of the old pessimist reactionaries. It is not
going to the Brave New World which Mr. Aldous Huxley described
with detestation, any more than to the New Utopia which Mr. H. G.
Wells described with delight. The world is what the saints and the
prophets saw it was; it is not merely getting better or merely getting
worse; there is one thing that the world does; it wobbles. Left to

---

[21] Horatio Herbert Kitchener (1850–1916) was an English field marshal and secretary of state for war in World War I. At the outbreak of the war, his appeals raised
thousands of patriotic volunteers.

[22] Engelbert Dollfuss (1892–1934), an Austrian statesman, was the leader of the
Christian Socialist party and became chancellor in 1932. In 1933 he suspended parliamentary government, crushed the socialists. In 1934 he was murdered by the Nazis.

itself, it does not get anywhere; though if helped by real reformers of the right religion and philosophy, it may get better in many respects, and sometimes for considerable periods. But in itself it is not a progress; it is not even a process; it is the fashion of this world that passeth away. Life in itself is not a ladder; it is a see-saw.

Now that is fundamentally what the Church has always said; and for about four hundred years has been more and more despised for saying. The Church never said that wrongs could not or should not be righted; or that commonwealths could not or should not be made happier; or that it was not worth while to help them in secular and material things; or that it is not a good thing if manners become milder, or comforts more common, or cruelties more rare. But she did say that we must not count on the certainty even of comforts becoming more common or cruelties more rare; as if this were an inevitable social trend towards a sinless humanity; instead of being as it was a mood of man, and perhaps a better mood, possibly to be followed by a worse one. We must not hate humanity, or despise humanity, or refuse to help humanity; but we must not trust humanity; in the sense of trusting a trend in human nature which cannot turn back to bad things. "Put not your trust in princes; nor in any child of man." [23] That is the precise point of this very practical sort of politics. Be a Royalist if you like (and there is a vast amount to be said, and a vast amount being said, just now, for more personal and responsible rule); try a Monarchy if you think it will be better; but do not trust a Monarchy, in the sense of expecting that a monarch will be anything but a man. Be a Democrat if you like (and I shall always think it the most generous and the most fundamentally Christian ideal in politics); express your sense of human dignity in manhood suffrage or any other form of equality; but put not your trust in manhood suffrage or in any child of man. There is one little defect about Man, the image of God, the wonder of the world and the paragon of animals; that he is not to be trusted. If you identify him with some ideal, which you choose to think is his inmost nature

[23] The quotation is from Psalms 146:3.

or his only goal, the day will come when he will suddenly seem to you a traitor.

He seems a traitor to-day to all that world of liberal and enlightened opinion, which had made up its mind about the way the world was going, in the path of progress and of peace; the world of Wells and Webb[24] and the Pacifists of America and the social reformers of Cambridge. Most of them are reduced to muttering, like the villain in the old melodrama, "a time will come." But it is in a very different tone from that in which they were crying quite lately, like the man in the comic song, "Now we shan't be long!" The most hopeful of them admit that we shall probably be very long, in reversing all that the reaction in Europe has done already. If, that is, it is ever reversed; and these people really have nothing except a purely mystical faith to suggest that it ever will be reversed. I am really more hopeful in being what they would call more hopeless; for I suspect that pretty nearly everything is eventually reversed. But it was exactly because they would not see this, that they were startled when their own reform or revolution was reversed before their own eyes. The point here, however, is that if there is something stable and not subject to reversal, it is not like anything that they imagine. Its habitation is not in the future or necessarily in any development of ideas peculiar to the present; we are not at the beginning of any endless and expanding dawn, but only of the ordinary daily dawns each followed by its own darkness; and the Faith, as Mr. Belloc said, "is the only beacon in this night, if beacon there be."

In the heart of Christendom, in the head of the Church, in the centre of the civilisation called Catholic, there and in no movement and in no future, is found that crystallisation of commonsense and true traditions and rational reforms, for which the modern man mistakenly looked to the whole trend of the modern age. From this will come the reminders that mercy is being neglected or memory cast away, and not from the men who happen to make the next batch of rulers on this restless and distracted earth. That is the fact

---

[24] Sidney Webb (1859–1947) was a prominent figure in the founding of the Fabian Society and in the development of socialist thought in England.

that we have all found at last; and that is why I have put it first. It is not the first in order, but it is the first in importance, of the facts I have discovered after I had discovered the truth; and if I had still been out in the darkness, it would in this dark hour have brought me to the door.

III. The Surrender upon Sex

I have explained that these are sketches of six separate occasions, on which I should have become a Catholic, if I had not been the one and only kind of human being who cannot become a Catholic. The excitement of conversion is still open to the atheist and the diabolist; and everybody can be converted except the convert. In my first outline, I mentioned that one of the crises, which would in any case have driven me the way I had gone already, was the shilly-shallying and sham liberality of the famous Lambeth Report on what is quaintly called Birth Control. It is in fact, of course, a scheme for preventing birth in order to escape control. But this particular case was only the culmination of a long process of compromise and cowardice about the problem of sex; the final surrender after a continuous retreat.

There is one historical human fact which now seems to me so plain and solid, that I think that even if I were to lose the Faith, I could not lose sight of the fact. It has rather the character of a fact of chemistry or geology; though from another side it is mysterious enough, like many other manifest and unmistakable facts. It is this: that at the moment when Religion lost touch with Rome, it changed instantly and internally, from top to bottom, in its very substance and the stuff of which it was made. It changed in substance; it did not necessarily change in form or features or externals. It might do the same things; but it could not be the same thing. It might go on saying the same things; but it was not the same thing that was saying them. At the very beginning, indeed, the situation was almost exactly like that. Henry VIII was a Catholic in everything except that he was not a Catholic. He observed everything down to the last bead and candle; he accepted everything down to the last deduction from a definition; he accepted everything except Rome. And in that instant of refusal, his religion became a different religion; a different sort of religion; a different sort of thing. In that instant it began to change; and it has not stopped changing yet. We are all somewhat wearily aware that some Modern Churchmen call such continuous change progress; as when we remark that a corpse crawling with worms has an increased vitality; or that a snow-man, slowly turning into a puddle, is purifying itself of its accretions. But I am not concerned with this argument here. The point is that a dead man may look like a sleeping man a moment after he is dead; but decomposition has actually begun. The point is that the snow-man may in theory be made in the real image of man. Michelangelo made a statue in snow; and it might quite easily have been an exact replica of one of his statues in marble; but it was not in marble. Most probably the snow-man has begun to melt almost as soon as it is made. But even if the frost holds, it is still a stuff capable of melting when the frost goes. It seemed to many that Protestantism would long continue to be, in the popular phrase, a perfect frost. But that does not alter the difference between ice and marble; and marble does not melt.

The same sort of progressives are always telling us to have a trust in the Future. As a fact, the one thing that a progressive cannot possibly have is a trust in the Future. He cannot have a trust in his own Future; let alone in his own Futurism. If he sets no limit to change, it may change all his own progressive views as much as his conservative views. It was so with the Church first founded by Henry VIII; who was, in almost everything commonly cursed as Popery, rather more Popish than the Pope. He thought he might trust it to go on being orthodox; to go on being sacramentalist; to go on being sacerdotalist; to go on being ritualist, and the rest. There was only one little weakness. It could not trust itself to go on being itself. Nothing else, except the Faith, can trust itself to go on being itself.

Now touching this truth in relation to Sex, I may be permitted to introduce a trivial journalistic anecdote. A few years before the War, some of my fellow-journalists, Socialists as well as Tories, were questioning me about what I really meant by Democracy; and especially if I really thought there was anything in Rousseau's ideal of the General Will. I said I thought (and I think I still think) that there can be such a thing, but it must be much more solid and unanimous than a mere majority, such as rules in party politics. I applied the old phrase of the Man in the Street, by saying that if I looked out of the window at a strange man walking past my house, I could bet heavily on his thinking some things, but not the common controversial things. The Liberals might have a huge majority, but he need not be a Liberal; statistics might prove England to be preponderantly Conservative, but I would not bet a button that he would be Conservative. But (I said) I should bet that he believes in wearing clothes. And my Socialist questioners did not question this; they, too, accepted clothes as so universal an agreement of common sense and civilisation, that we might attribute the tradition to a total stranger, unless he were a lunatic. Such a little while ago! To-day, when I see the stranger walking down the street, I should not bet that he believes even in clothes. The country is dotted with Nudist Colonies; the bookstalls are littered with Nudist magazines; the papers swarm with polite little paragraphs, praising the brownness and braveness of the special sort of anarchical asses here in question. At any given moment, there may be a General Will; but it is an uncommonly weak and wavering sort of will, without the Faith to support it.

As in that one matter of modesty, or the mere externals of sex, so in all the deeper matters of sex, the modern will has been amazingly weak and wavering. And I suppose it is because the Church has known from the first this weakness which we have all discovered at last, that about certain sexual matters She has been very decisive and dogmatic; as many good people have quite honestly thought, too decisive and dogmatic. Now a Catholic is a person who has plucked up courage to face the incredible and inconceivable idea that something else may be wiser than he is. And the most striking and outstanding illustration is perhaps to be found in the Catholic view of marriage as compared with the modern theory of divorce; not, it must be noted, the *very* modern theory of divorce, which is the mere negation of marriage; but even more the slightly less modern and more moderate theory of divorce, which was generally accepted even when I was a boy. This is the very vital point or test of the question; for it explains the Church's rejection of the moderate as well as the immoderate theory. It illustrates the very fact I am pointing out, that Divorce has already turned into something totally different from what was intended, even by those who first proposed it. Already we must think ourselves back into a different world of thought, in order to understand how anybody ever thought it was compatible with Victorian virtue; and many very virtuous Victorians did. But they only tolerated this social solution as an exception; and many other modern social solutions they would not have tolerated at all. My own parents were not even orthodox Puritans or High Church people; they were Universalists more akin to Unitarians. But they would have regarded Birth-Prevention exactly as they would have regarded Infanticide. Yet about Divorce such liberal Protestants did hold an intermediate view, which was substantially this. They thought the normal necessity and duty of all married people was to remain faithful to their marriage; that this could be demanded of them, like common honesty or any other virtue. But they thought that in some very extreme and extraordinary cases a divorce was allowable. Now, putting aside our own mystical and sacramental doctrine, this was not, on the face of it, an unreasonable position. It certainly was not meant to be an anarchical position. But the Catholic Church, standing almost alone, declared that it would in fact lead to an anarchical position; and the Catholic Church was right.

Any man with eyes in his head, whatever the ideas in his head, who looks at the world as it is to-day, must know that the whole social substance of marriage has changed; just as the whole social substance of Christianity changed with the divorce of Henry VIII. As in the other case, the externals remained for a time and some of them remain still. Some divorced persons, who can be married quite legally by a registrar, go on complaining bitterly that they cannot be married by a priest. They regard a church as a peculiarly suitable place in which to make and break the same vow at the same moment. And the Bishop of London, who was supposed to sympathise with the more sacramental party, recently submitted to such a demand on the ground that it was a special case. As if every human being's case were not a special case. That decision was one of the occasions on which I should have done a bolt, if I had delayed it so long. But the general social atmosphere is much the most important matter. Numbers of normal people are getting married, thinking already that they may be divorced. The instant that idea enters, the whole conception of the old Protestant compromise vanishes. The sincere and innocent Victorian would never have married a woman reflecting that he could divorce her. He would as soon have married a woman reflecting that he could murder her. These things were not supposed to be among the daydreams of the honeymoon. The psychological substance of the whole thing has altered; the marble has turned to ice; and the ice has melted with most amazing rapidity. The Church was right to refuse even the exception. The world has admitted the exception; and the exception has become the rule.

As I have said, the weak and inconclusive pronouncement upon Birth-Prevention was only the culmination of this long intellectual corruption. I need not discuss the particular problem again at this point; beyond saying that the same truth applies as in the case of Divorce. People propose an easy way out of certain human responsibilities and difficulties; including a way out of the responsibility and difficulty of doing economic justice and achieving better payment for the poor. But these people propose this easy method, in the hope that some people will only use it to a moderate extent; whereas it is much more probable that an indefinite number will use it to an indefinite extent. It is odd that they do not see this; because the writers and thinkers among them are no longer by any means optimistic about human nature, like Rousseau; but much more pessimistic about human nature than we are. Considering mankind as described, for instance, by Mr. Aldous Huxley, it is hard to see what answer he could possibly give, except the answer which we give, if the question were put thus: "On the one side, there is an easy way out of the difficulty by avoiding childbirth; on the other side, there is a very difficult way out of the difficulty, by reconstructing the whole social system and toiling and perhaps fighting for the better system. Which way are the men you describe more likely to take?" But my concern is not with open and direct opponents like Mr. Huxley; but with all to whom I might once have looked to defend the country of the Christian altars. They ought surely to know that the foe now on the frontiers offers no terms of compromise; but threatens a complete destruction. And they have sold the pass.

IV. The Prayer-Book Problem

One of the events which would have made me a Catholic, if I had not already been a Catholic, was the curious affair of the New Prayer-Book. It revealed to me a reality I had not hitherto realised. There really was a Church of England; or rather there really was an England which largely imagined that it possessed and controlled a Church. But this Church was not the Church I thought I had belonged to; the keen, cultivated and sincere group of men who claimed to be Catholic. It was a much vaster and vaguer background of men; who did not believe in anything in particular, but who claimed to be Protestant. But the vital point was that, whether they claimed to be Protestants or clamorously bragged of being atheists, they all seemed to have this fixed idea; that they owned the Church of England; and could turn it into a Mormon temple if they liked. I could not, in any case, have gone on being owned in that way.

But in order to understand all that was involved, it is necessary to say a word about the Anglican Prayer-Book itself. The Book of Common Prayer is the masterpiece of Protestantism. It is more so than the work of Milton. It is the one positive possession and attraction; the one magnet and talisman for people even outside the Anglican Church, as are the great Gothic cathedrals for people outside the Catholic Church. I can speak, I think, for many other converts, when I say that the only thing that can produce any sort of nostalgia or romantic regret, any shadow of homesickness in one who has in truth come home, is the rhythm of Cranmer's prose. All the other supposed superiorities of any sort of Protestantism are quite ficti-tious. Tell a Catholic convert that he has lost his liberty, and he will laugh. A distinguished literary lady wrote recently that I had entered the most restricted of all Christian communions, and I was mon-strously amused. A Catholic has fifty times more feeling of being free than a man caught in the net of the nervous compromises of

Anglicanism; just as a man considering all England feels more free than a man obeying the Whips of one particular party. He has the range of two thousand years full of twelve-hundred thousand controversies, thrashed out by thinker against thinker, school against school, guild against guild, nation against nation, with no limit except the fundamental logical fact that the things were worth arguing, because they could be ultimately solved and settled. As for Reason, our monopoly is practically admitted in the modern world. Except for one or two dingy old atheists in Fleet Street[25] (for whom I have great sympathy), nothing except Rome now defends the reliability of Reason. Much stronger is the appeal of unreason; or of that beauty which perhaps is beyond reason. The English Litany, the music and the magic of the great sixteenth-century style—*that* does call a man backwards like the song of the sirens; as Virgil and the poets might have called to a Pagan who had entered the Early Church. Only, being a Romanist and therefore a Rationalist, he does not go back; he naturally does not forget everything else, because his opponents four hundred years ago had a stylistic knack which they have now entirely lost. For the Anglicans cannot do the trick now, any more than anybody else. Modern prayers, and theirs perhaps more than any, seem to be perfectly incapable of avoiding journalese. And the Prayer-Book prose seems to follow them like a derisive echo. Lambeth or Convocation will publish a prayer saying something like, "Guide us, O Lord, to the solution of our social problems"; and the great organ of old will groan in the background.... "All who are desolate and oppressed." The first Anglicans asked for peace and happiness, truth and justice; but nothing can stop the latest Anglicans, and many others, from the horrid habit of asking for improvement in international relations.

But *why* has the old Protestant Prayer-Book a power like that of great poetry upon the spirit and the heart? The reason is much deeper than the mere avoidance of journalese. It might be put in a sentence; it has style; it has tradition; it has religion; it was written by apostate Catholics. It is strong, not in so far as it is the first Protestant

---

[25] Fleet Street was the locus of the newspaper publishing industry in London.

book, but in so far as it was the last Catholic book. As it happens, this can be proved in the most practical manner from the actual details of the prose. The most moving passages in the old Anglican Prayer-Book are exactly those that are least like the atmosphere of the Anglicans. They are moving, or indeed thrilling, precisely because they say the things which Protestants have long left off saying; and which only Catholics still say. Anybody who knows anything of literature knows when a style lifts itself to its loftiest efforts; and in these cases it is always to say strongly what we still endeavour to say, however weakly; but which nobody else ever endeavours to say at all. Let anyone recall for himself the very finest passages in the Book of Common Prayer, and he will soon see that they are concerned specially with spiritual thoughts and themes that now seem strange and terrible; but anyhow, the reverse of common; ". . . in the hour of death and in the day of Judgment." Who talks about the hour of death? Who talks about the Day of Judgment? Only a litter of shabby little priests from the Italian Mission. Not certainly the popular and eloquent Dean of Bumblebury, who is so Broad and yet so High. Certainly not the charming and fashionable Vicar of St. Ethelbald's, who is so High and yet so Broad. Still less the clergyman helping in the same parish, who is frankly Low. It is the same on every page, where that spirit inspires that style. "Suffer us not, for any pains of death, to fall from Thee." . . . "Ah, that's what gets you" (or words to that effect), as Lord Peter Wimsey truly said of this phrase, in the detective tale of Miss Dorothy Sayers;[26] who, like Lord Peter, knows a good deal about other things besides poisons; and understands her hero's historical traditions very well. But did you ever hear the curate fresh from the cricket-field, or the vicar smiling under the Union Jacks of the Conservative Rally, dwell upon that penultimate peril; or the danger of falling from God amid the pains of death? Very morbid. Just like those Dago devotional books. So very *Roman*.

I do not think the old Anglo-Catholics who were my friends, or the many who are still my friends, would deny that there has been

[26] Dorothy Sayers (1893–1957) was an English author of detective stories (featuring Lord Peter Wimsey), a playwright and a translator of Dante.

a modern vulgarisation of religion, largely through the spread of this official optimism. But though they themselves are often quite free from the vulgar form of it, they could hardly deny that it is largely official and very widely spread. Yet it came as a great shock to me to discover how official and widespread it was. I had exaggerated the importance of an intelligent minority, because it was important to me. But the public and the world without were given up to Arian and Pelagian[27] demagogues like Dean Inge and Dr. Barnes; and a sort of negative Protestantism could still sweep the field. It swept the whole field in the matter of the Prayer-Book. The proposal of an amended Prayer-Book, or rather two alternative Prayer-Books, was not decided for the Church by the Church; or by the communicants; or by the congregation. It was settled by a mob of politicians, atheists, agnostics, dissenters, Parsees; avowed enemies of that Church or of any Church, who happened to have M.P. after their names. If the whole thing had any historic motto, or deserved anything higher than a headline, what was written across all that Anglican story was not *Ecclesia Anglicana*, or *Via Media*,[28] or anything of the sort; it was *Cujus Regio Ejus Religio*;[29] or rendering unto Cæsar the things that are God's.

I add one incident to contrast Style, among men who had been Catholics for fourteen-hundred years, with that among men who have been Protestants for four-hundred years. A Protestant organisation presented all the atheists, etc., who had voted Protestant, with a big black Bible or Prayer-Book, or both, decorated outside with a picture of the Houses of Parliament. *In hoc signo vinces*.[30] It would be

---

[27] Arianism and Pelagianism were both early Christian heresies. Arianism, which flourished in the early fourth century, viewed Christ as a lesser being than God the Father. Pelagianism, which arose in the late fourth century, rejected the doctrine of original sin and contended that the human will is capable of good without the aid of divine grace.

[28] *Via media* was the Anglican "middle way" between the Catholicism of Rome and the Calvinism of Geneva.

[29] The Latin phrase *cujus regio ejus religio* means "whose the region, his the religion".

[30] *In hoc signo vinces* is Latin for "In this sign you shall conquer", the words the Emperor Constantine saw, along with a cross, in the sky before the battle of Milvian Bridge in 312.

very idolatrous to put a cross or crucifix outside a book; but a picture of Parliament where the Party Funds are kept, and the peerages sold ———. That is the temple where dwell the gods of Israel.... We know the world progresses, and education is certainly extended, and there are fewer illiterates; and I suppose it is all right. But those four strong centuries of Protestant England begin with a Book of Common Prayer, in which, even amid the treachery and panic of Cranmer, and in the very moment of men rending themselves from Rome and Christendom, they could lift in such sublime language so authentic a cry of Christian men: "By Thy precious death and burial; by Thy glorious resurrection and ascension; and by the coming of the Holy Ghost." Those centuries begin with that speech of men still by instinct and habit of mind Catholic; and the Protestant civilization evolves and the education spreads, and widens in wealth and power and towns and colleges; until at last the ripe and final fruit of its culture is produced, in the form of a fat black book of a cushiony sort, with a real photo-view, a view of one of the Sights, nicely tucked in to its neat black padded binding or frame.... A Present from Ramsgate ... anyhow, four-hundred years march from Rome.

V. The Collapse of Materialism

Some little time ago Dr. David Forsyth delivered to the Section of Psychiatry (Royal Society of Medicine) an address which was certainly a psychological curiosity; of considerable interest to psychologists, pathologists, alienists and all other students of the mental breakdown in the modern world. It was a perfect and compact illustration of the very common combination of a superiority complex with arrested development, and inhibitions on almost all forms of intelligent curiosity. But I mention it here, not because of its narrowness, but of its direct negation of all that is really new in scientific discovery. It is no news to us that a materialist can be bigoted; but we do not always come upon so startling an example of his being antiquated.

It is not worth while to take any particular notice of all the diseased stuff about sadism and masochism being the sources of religion. We may note in passing, with a rather dreary amusement, that this sort of writer can never sustain a connected train of thought; and that he gets even these dismal technical terms hopelessly entangled; for he declares that Islam stands for sadism and Christendom for masochism, having just argued that the Christian persecution of heretics was typically sadistic. But all this judgment of great human events, good or bad, in terms of some obscure streak of lunacy, is itself an amusement for lunatics. It is exactly as if a man were to argue: "There is a special sort of madman who thinks he is made of glass; I will call this disease Vitreosity; and I will then show that anybody anywhere, who for any reason had anything to do with glass was a victim of vitreosity. The desert-merchants who were said to have invented glass, the medieval craftsmen who so successfully coloured glass, the early astronomers who first fitted telescopes with lenses of glass, all showed Vitreosity in various stages of that disease; it is akin to subconscious *libido* because Peeping Tom looked through a window, which may have been made of glass; it is the root impulse of alcoholism, because people drink out of glasses; and Prince Albert and Queen Victoria were obviously stricken with raving and uncontrolled Vitreosity; because they built the Crystal Palace."[31] The slight defect in this theory (which is quite as scientific as Dr. Forsyth's) is that in order to theorise, it is sometimes useful to think. It is obvious that all these people had a thousand other reasons for doing all they did, besides being mad on glass; and it is equally obvious that the great religions, true or false, had a thousand reasons for doing all they did, without being mad on masochism or sadism.

Only, as I say, we may well emerge from this slime and consider the real case of Dr. Forsyth, and his strange ignorance of the very elements of modern thought, and even rather specially of modern science. Now on the larger matter, his thesis was essentially this; that science and religion, so far from being reconciled or even reconcilable, were divided by the vital contradiction that science belongs to what he called "reality-thinking," or we call objective truth; while

---

[31] The Crystal Palace was a vast building erected in London in 1851 to house the first international exhibition of the products and machines of the industrial age.

religion belonged to what he called "pleasure-thinking," or what most people call imagination. I need not mention the hundred obvious objections to this crude division; as, for instance, that religion has not confined itself to imagining pleasurable things, but has often been blamed by people like Dr. Forsyth for imagining unpleasant ones; or that it is arguing in a circle to prove at the end that religion is inconsistent with science merely by assuming at the beginning that it is inconsistent with truth. I am only concerned here to insist, not merely that the view is the reverse of the truth, but that the view is actually the very reverse of the modern view.

If there are two staring and outstanding facts about science and religion at this particular moment, they are these. First, that science is claiming much less than it did to show us a solid and objective reality. And second, that religion is claiming much *more* than it did (at least for centuries past) that its miracles and marvels of mystical experience can be proved to exist as a solid and objective reality. On the one side, the Atom has entirely lost the objective solidity it had for the nineteenth-century materialists. On the other side, the Ascension is accepted as a case of Levitation by many who would not accept it as an Ascension. On the one hand, the science of physics has almost become a science of metaphysics. For it is not merely, as is often said, that the Atom has become an abstract mathematical formula; it is almost as true to say that it has become a mere algebraic symbol. For the new physicists tell us frankly that what they describe is *not* the objective reality of the thing they observe; that they are not examining an object as the nineteenth century materialists thought they were examining an object. Some of them tell us that they are only observing certain disturbances or distortions, actually created by their own attempt to observe. Eddington[32] is more agnostic about the material world than Huxley ever was about the spiritual world. A very unfortunate moment at which to say that science deals directly with reality and objective truth.

[32] Sir Arthur Stanley Eddington (1882–1944) was an English astronomer and popularizer of modern theories of physics. He became director of the Royal Observatory in Greenwich in 1914.

On the other hand, on the other plane, the plane of historical and practical argument, it is the very moment at which religion really is appealing to reality and objective truth. The Church throws down the unanswered challenge of Lourdes; the Spiritualists positively claim to prove their new religion by experiments, like a thesis in chemistry or electricity; and a vast number of independent intellectuals, who are neither Catholics nor Spiritualists, have begun to show an entirely new interest in the logical, or even the legal case for some of the great historic miracles. For instance, there have been two or three books following on the line of the brilliant but strictly scientific book called *Who Moved the Stone*; and the tendency of the most detached writers is to admit more and more that the evidence for such events has been underrated. The youngest school of Catholic apologists, such as Father Knox and Mr. Christopher Hollis and Mr. Arnold Lunn,[33] attack almost entirely with the weapons of proof and practical evidence; and it is no longer pretended that they always have the worst of it. A very unfortunate moment at which to say that religion deals only with pleasant fancies and imaginations.

Dr. Forsyth's antiquated style of thought interests me here, however, only as drawing attention to the familiar modern facts of which he seems never to have heard. And most relevant here is the fact of that extraordinary scientific change in the attitude to facts. It has its place in this series, because it is one of the great changes which had not developed in any full and public fashion, even by the time that I finally sought admission to the Church; and, at the much earlier time when I had already begun to think about it, all the popular science that a layman heard of was dominated by the now dead materialism of Haeckel.[34] It is, therefore, true to say that this huge revolution in the philosophy of physical science was one of the world events which came after my conversion; but would have hugely hastened it, if it had come before my conversion. Only the exact nature

[33] Arnold Lunn (1886–1974) was an English writer and convert to Catholicism.
[34] Ernst Haeckel (1834–1919) was a German scientist and champion of Darwinism against religious orthodoxy.

of the effect, of this scientific revolution upon personal religion, is often misstated and widely misunderstood.

It is not, as some seem to fancy, that we think there is anything particularly Christian about electrons, any more than there is anything essentially atheistic about atoms. It is not that we propose to base our philosophy on their physics; any more than to base our ancient theology on their most recent biology. We are not "going to the country" with a set of slogans or party-cries, like *Electrons for the Elect*, or *For Priest and Proton*. The catastrophic importance for Catholics, of this collapse of materialism, is simply the fact that the most confident cosmic statements of science can collapse. If fifty years hence the electron is as entirely exploded as the atom, it will not affect us; for we have never founded our philosophy on the electron any more than on the atom. But the materialists did found *their* philosophy on the atom. And it is quite likely that some spiritual fad or other is at this moment being founded on the electron. To a man of my generation, the importance of the change does not consist in its destroying the dogma (which was after all a detail, though a very dogmatic dogma), "Matter consists of indivisible atoms." But it does consist in its destroying the accepted, universal and proclaimed and popularised dogma: "You must accept the conclusions of science." Scores and hundreds of times I have heard, through my youth and early manhood, the repetition of that ultimatum: "You must accept the conclusions of science." And it is that notion or experience that has now been concluded; or rather excluded. Whatever else is questionable, there is henceforth no question of anybody "accepting" the conclusions of science. The new scientists themselves do not ask us to accept the conclusions of science. The new scientists themselves do not accept the conclusions of the new science. To do them justice, they deny vigorously that science has concluded; or that it has, in that sense, any conclusion. The finest intellects among them repeat, again and again, that science is inconclusive.

Which is all very well, and all very wise, and all very true to the gradual adjustment of truths on their own plane. But meanwhile— there is such a thing as human life. The Victorian agnostics waited hopefully for science to give them a working certainty about life. The new physicist philosophers are in no way different, except that they wait hopelessly instead of hopefully. For they know very well the real meaning of relativity; that their own views may pass from being relatively right to being relatively wrong. And meanwhile, as I say, there is such a thing as wanting a working rule as to whether we should pay our debts or murder our enemies. We would not wait for a nineteenth-century enlightenment that might come. We certainly will not wait for a twentieth-century enlightenment that cannot come. If we want a guide to life, it seems that we must look elsewhere.

VI. The Case of Spain

The point of the recent political story in Spain has never been put clearly in the English papers; perhaps not quite clearly even in the Catholic papers. It is a very striking example of how the world has really moved, since my own most important change of conviction occurred. There is a paradox in every story of conversion; which is perhaps the reason why the records of it are never ideally satisfactory. It is in its very nature the extinction of egoism; and yet every account of it must sound egoistic. It means, at least in the case of the Religion in question, a recognition of reality which has nothing to do with relativity. It is as if a man said, "This inn really exists, even if I have never found it"; or, "My home is actually in this village; and would be there, if I had never reached it." It is the recognition that the truth is true, apart from the truth-seeker; and yet the description must be the autobiography of a truth-seeker; generally a rather depressing sort of person. It will therefore sound egotistical, if I preface these remarks by saying that I was for a long time a Liberal in the sense of belonging to the Liberal Party. I am still a Liberal; it is only the Liberal Party that has disappeared. I understood its ideal to be that of equal citizenship and personal freedom; and they are my own political ideals to this day. The point here, however, is that I worked for a long time with the practical organization of Liberalism; I wrote for a great part of my life for the old *Daily News*; and I knew of course that it identified political liberty, rightly or wrongly, with representative government. Then came the breach, on which I need not insist; except by saying that I became quite convinced of two facts. First, that representative government had ceased to be representative. Second, that Parliament was in fact gravely menaced by political corruption. Politicians did not represent the populace, even the most noisy and vulgar of the populace. Politicians did not deserve the dignified name of demagogues. They deserved no name except perhaps the name of bagmen; they were travelling for private firms. If they represented anything, it was vested interests, vulgar but not even popular.

For this reason, when the Fascists' revolt appeared in Italy, I could not be entirely hostile to it; for I knew the hypocritical plutocracy against which it rebelled. But neither could I be entirely friendly to it; for I believed in the civic equality in which the politicians pretended to believe. For the present purpose, the problem can be put very briefly. The whole of the real case for Fascism can be put in two words never printed in our newspapers: *secret societies*. The whole case against Fascism could be put in one word now never used and almost forgotten: *legitimacy*. For the first, the Fascist was justified in smashing the politicians; for their contract with the people was secretly contradicted by their secret contracts with gangs and conspiracies. For the second, Fascism could never be quite satisfactory; for it did not rest on authority but only on power; which is the weakest thing in the world. The Fascists said in effect, "We may not be the majority, but we are the most vigorous and intelligent minority." Which is simply challenging any other intelligent minority to show that it is more vigorous. It may well end in the very anarchy it attempted to avoid. Compared with this, despotism and democracy are *legitimate*. I mean there is no doubt about who is the King's eldest son or about who has most votes in the most mechanical election. But a mere competition of intelligent minorities is a rather dreadful prospect. That, it seems to me, is a fair statement of the case for and against the Fascist movement. And now I should like to apply it to the curious case of Spain; and note how Liberalism met the issue.

For weeks and months on end my old organ the *Daily News* (now the *News-Chronicle*) had warned the public of all these doubtful and dangerous implications of Fascism. It had reviled Fascism for its vices;

and rather more virulently for its virtues. But anyhow it had furiously
denounced the notion of a minority imposing its will by mere violence, by weapons or military training, in contempt of the constitutional democracy in which the people expressed its will through
Parliament. I think there is a great deal to be said for that view; especially in England, where Parliament is really normal and national as it
never was in Italy or Germany. I could write much for and much against
the Liberal theory as enunciated in the *News-Chronicle*. And then, suddenly, the whole case was thrown over, and turned upside down, in
face of the simple situation in Spain.

First it must be remembered that the Church is always in advance
of the world. That is why it is said to be behind the times. It
discussed everything so long ago that people have forgotten the discussion. St. Thomas was an internationalist before all our inter-
nationalists; St. Joan was a nationalist almost before there were nations;
Blessed Robert Bellarmine[35] said all there is to be said for democracy before any ordinary worldling dared to be a democrat; and (what
is to the purpose here) the Christian social reform was in full activity *before* any of these quarrels of Fascists and Bolshevists appeared.
The Popular Party was working out the ideas of Leo XIII[36] before
a single Blackshirt had been seen in Italy. The same popular ideals
had been moving in Spain; with the result that they had really become
popular. There were other complications, of course; the Court had
never been quite popular; the Dictatorship had not, I think, been
imaginative about the curious problem of Catalonia;[37] but all this
did not effect the profound and popular Catholic change. The Pope
particularly insisted that he had no objection to the Republic as
such; there was no opposition to anything but to certain inhuman
ideals, by which men would lose humanity in losing personal liberty

---

[35] Robert Bellarmine (1542–1621) was an Italian cardinal known for his polemics
against Protestantism and for his defense of the temporal power of the pope.

[36] The Popular Party, or *Partito Popolare*, was an Italian Catholic political party
founded in 1919. Pope Leo XIII reigned from 1878 to 1903. His encyclical *Rerum
novarum* (1891) supported the rights of labor, called for a just wage and defended
trade unions.

[37] Catalonia is a region in the northeastern corner of Spain that was involved in a
long and constant struggle with its neighbors to maintain political and cultural autonomy.

and property. Well, in the perfectly fair and open intellectual inter-
change, in which all Liberals are supposed to believe, the Catholic
ideals won. At an entirely peaceful and legal election, exactly like
any English election, a vast majority voted in various degrees for
the traditional truths, which had been normal to the Nation for
much more than a thousand years. Spain spoke; if indeed elections
do speak; and declared constitutionally against Communism, against
Atheism, against the negation that starved normality in our time.
Nobody said that this majority had been achieved by military violence. Nobody pretended that an armed minority had imposed it
on the State. If the Liberal theory of Parliamentary majorities was
just, this was just. If the Parliamentary system was a popular system, this was popular. And then the Socialists suddenly jumped up
and did exactly everything that the Fascists have been blamed for
doing. They used bombs and guns and instruments of violence to
prevent the fulfilment of the will of the people, or at least of the
will of the Parliament. Having lost the game by the rules of democracy, they tried to win it after all entirely by the rules of war; in
this case of Civil War. They tried to overthrow a pacific Parliament by a militarist *coup d'état*. In short, they behaved exactly like
Mussolini; or rather they did the very worst that has ever been
attributed to Mussolini; and without a rag of his theoretical excuse.

And what did Liberalism say? What did my dear old friends of
liberty and peaceful citizenship say? Naturally, I assumed on opening the paper that it would rally to the defence of Parliament and
peaceful representative government and rebuke the attempt to make
a minority dominant by mere military violence. Judge of my aston-
ishment, when I found Liberals lamenting aloud over the unfortunate failure of these Socialistic Fascists to reverse the result of a General
Election. I had been a Liberal in the old Liberal days; we were not
unacquainted with Tory and Unionist victories at the polls; we had
often gone contentedly into Opposition. It had never been suggested that when Balfour or Baldwin[38] constitutionally became

---

[38] Arthur James, Earl of Balfour (1848–1930), British prime minister from 1902 to
1905, authored books on religion and philosophy. Stanley Baldwin (1867–1947) was
a three-time Conservative British prime minister between the two world wars.

Prime Ministers, all the Nonconformists should go out with guns
and bayonets to reverse the popular vote; or the Leader of the Opposition begin to throw dynamite at the elected Leader of the House.
The only inference was that Liberalism was only opposed to mili-
tarists when they were Fascists; and entirely approved of Fascists so
long as they were Socialists.

Now that is a small and purely political point. But to me it was
very awakening. It showed me quite clearly the fundamental truth
of the modern world. And that is this: there are no Fascists; there
are no Socialists; there are no Liberals; there are no Parliamentarians. There is the one supremely inspiring and irritating institution
in the world; and there are its enemies. Its enemies are ready to be
for violence or against violence, for liberty or against liberty, for
representation or against representation; and even for peace or against
peace. It gave me an entirely new certainty, even in the practical and
political sense, that I had chosen well.

VII. The Well and the Shallows

In numberless novels and newspaper articles, we have all read about
a process which is still apparently regarded as novel or new; though
it has been described in almost exactly the same terms for nearly a
hundred years; and in slightly different terms for hundreds of years
before that. I mean what is called the growth of doubt or the
disturbance of faith; and the only point about it which is pertinent
here is this; that it is always described as a revolt of the deeper
parts of the mind against something that is comparatively superficial. We need not deny that modern doubt, like ancient doubt,
does ask deep questions; we only deny that, as compared with our
own philosophy, it gives any deeper answers. And it is a general
rule, touching what is called modern thought, that while the questions are often really deep, the answers are often decidedly shallow.
And it is perhaps even more important to remark that, while the
questions are in a sense eternal, the answers are in every sense
ephemeral. The world is still asking the questions that were asked

by Job. The world will not long be contented with the answers that are given by Joad.[39]

The chances of the Book of Joad being as permanent as the Book of Job are limited by certain perfectly practical calculations. Mr. Joad is an able and sincere man; and nobody doubts that his opinions are the product of his own mind; but they are very unmistakably the product of his own age. In this case it would be more correct to say, of his own generation. For the sceptics throughout the ages inherit nothing except a negation. Their positive policy or ideal varies, not only from century to century, but even from father to son. A free-thinker like Bradlaugh,[40] coming out of the individualistic nineteenth century and the mercantile spirit of the Midlands, was careful to explain that he was an Individualist. A free-thinker of the next generation, like Mr. Joseph McCabe,[41] was careful to explain that he was a Socialist. A free-thinker wanting to make a splash to-day would almost certainly insist that he was not a Socialist; which has come to mean something as mild as Mr. Ramsay MacDonald.[42] For those who can believe in each of these social moves in turn, as they happen to turn up, the matter may be irrelevant. But some of us will simply draw the moral which determines the whole question of this issue between the traditions of truth and doubt. Those who leave the tradition of truth do not escape into something which we call Freedom. They only escape into something else, which we call Fashion.

---

[39] Cyril Edwin Mitchinson Joad (1891–1953) was an English philosopher, author and teacher. A pacifist (he was a conscientious objector during World War I) and agnostic, he championed unpopular causes and wrote popular philosophical works; the *Book of Joad* is probably a reference to one or all of them. He won fame as a regular guest on the BBC radio program "Brain Trust".

[40] Charles Bradlaugh (1833–91) was an English journalist, politician and freethinker.

[41] Joseph McCabe (1867–1955) was the English founder of the Rationalist Press Association.

[42] James Ramsay MacDonald (1866–1937), leader of the Labour party in Britain from 1911 to 1914, was a pacifist by conviction and opposed England's participation in World War I. He lost leadership of the Labour party in 1914 and his seat in the House of Commons in 1918, though he regained both in 1922.

That is really the crux of the controversy between the two views of history and philosophy. If it were true that by leaving the temple we walked out into a world of truths, the question would be answered; but it is not true. By leaving the temple, we walk out into a world of idols; and the idols of the marketplace are more perishable and passing than the gods of the temple we have left. If we wished to test rationally the case of rationalism, we should follow the career of the sceptic and ask how far he remained sceptical about the idols or ideals of the world into which he went. There are very few sceptics in history who cannot be proved to have been instantly swallowed by some swollen convention or some hungry humbug of the hour, so that all their utterances about contemporary things now look to us almost pathetically contemporary. The little group of Atheists, who still run their paper in Fleet Street and frequently honour me with hearty but somewhat hasty denunciation, began their agitation in the old Victorian days, and selected for themselves a terrible appropriate title. They did not call themselves Atheists, they called themselves Secularists. Never was a more bitter and blighting confession made in the form of a boast. For the word "secular" does not mean anything so sensible as "worldly." It does not even mean anything so spirited as "irreligious." To be secular simply means to be of the age; that is, of the age which is passing; of the age which, in their case, is already passed. There is one tolerably correct translation of the Latin word which they have chosen as their motto. There is one adequate equivalent of the word "secular"; and it is the word "dated."

In the essays in this series, I have considered some of the effects of this continuous process of time and change, as it has affected the world, even after I myself ceased to look to its changes for essential guidance. I have noted that the changes, which continue to occur, point more and more to the truth of the unchanging philosophy which stands apart from them. I could add, of course, a long list of other examples of exactly the same truth. I could point, for instance, to the collapse of Prohibition; not so much in narrow sense of Prohibition as in the general sense of Prohibitionism. For what failed with the American experiment was not merely a particular chemical experiment with some alleged chemical constituent, which they chose to call alcohol. It was a whole attitude towards all the complex uses and abuses of human things. The great outstanding principle of the modern materialistic world has been Prohibition; even Prohibition in the abstract. Where we say that a social element is dangerous or doubtful, that it must be watched, that it may on due occasion be restrained, the thing that was called the Modern Mind always cried aloud with a voice of thunder that it must be forbidden. The Prohibitionist declares that there must be no wine; the Pacifist that there must be no war; the Communist that there must be no private property; the Secularist that there must be no religious worship. The failure of Prohibition in the one country in which it was a favourite, in which it was a popular idea in so far as anything so inhuman can be popular, was the collapse of the whole conception of wiping out entirely the temptations of man and the trials of mortal life. After that, it is tacitly agreed that there is no such simple way out of moral problems; it is almost admitted that they must be referred to the moral sense. We were actually driven back on the desperate and tragic duty of our fathers, of deciding for ourselves whether we were drinking too much, or whether we were fighting in a just quarrel, or whether we were only defending our own lawful property, or getting other people's property by lawless usury. Such a demand was naturally a great strain on the Modern Mind. For the Modern Mind is not at all accustomed to making up its mind. It finds the task almost as unfamiliar as working its own farm or practising its own craft; or doing a hundred other things, that human beings had done from the foundations of the world. In short, it would not accept the Catholic doctrine that human life is a battle; it only wanted to have it announced, from time to time in the newspapers, that it was a victory.

There are, I say, a number of other more general defeats of the attack on the Faith, on each of which it would be easy to write a long essay; the longer as the essential truth in the matter was more subtle and more universal. But I will close this series with the examples which I have given, because I think they suffice to show the general trend of the truth which I desire to suggest. The simplest summary of my meaning is to throw my mind back to all the things that seemed in my youth to be the rivals or reasonable alternatives to my religious conviction, and consider whether they could still play even the part which they did. The answer is that not one of them could now even remotely resemble a rival; or be even reasonable as an alternative. There was a time when men of my sympathies felt even tragically the quarrel between the Republic and the Church; the apparent misunderstanding between political equality and mystical authority. It is a commonplace to-day that the world has reacted much more against equality than against authority. But that in itself would not have disposed of the democratic ideals of any sincere democrat. It is the thing called democracy that has itself disappointed the democrat. However much I might hate the Fascists, heartily as I do indeed despise the Hitlerites, that would never restore the mere abstract faith in the Republicans. If I lost my religion to-morrow, I could not again believe that the mere fact of turning Kamchatka from a Monarchy to a Republic would solve all its social sins. I have seen too many Republicans, with their greasy platform promises and their guzzling secret societies. I can remember when being a Socialist was a real inspiration to youth; but anybody who thinks it could be an inspiration to the more elderly phase of maturity, has only to look at the more elderly Socialists. In short, the point I mentioned at the beginning of this article is the point of the whole matter; that while the questions are still deep and tragic enough, the recent answers have not really been revolutionary, but only superficial. I could not abandon the faith, without falling back on something more shallow than the faith. I could not cease to be a Catholic, except by becoming something more narrow than a Catholic. A man must narrow his mind in order to lose the universal philosophy; everything that has happened up to this very day has confirmed this conviction; and whatever happens tomorrow will confirm it anew. We have come out of the shallows and the dry places to the one deep well; and the Truth is at the bottom of it.

THE RETURN TO RELIGION

In the days when Huxley and Herbert Spencer and the Victorian agnostics were trumpeting as a final truth the famous hypothesis of Darwin, it seemed to thousands of simple people almost impossible that religion should survive. It is all the more ironic that it has not only survived them all, but it is a perfect example (perhaps the only real example) of what they called the Survival of the Fittest.

It so happens that it does really and truly fit in with the theory offered by Darwin; which was something totally different from most of the theories accepted by Darwinians. This real original theory of Darwin has since very largely broken down in the general field of biology and botany; but it does actually apply to this particular argument in the field of religious history. The recent re-emergence of our religion is a survival of the fittest as Darwin meant it, and not as popular Darwinism meant it; so far as it meant anything. Among the innumerable muddles, which mere materialistic fashion made out of the famous theory, there was in many quarters a queer idea that the Struggle for Existence was of necessity an actual struggle between the candidates for survival; literally a cut-throat competition. There was a vague idea that the strongest creature violently crushed the others. And the notion that this was the one method of improvement came everywhere as good news to bad men; to bad rulers, to bad employers, to swindlers and sweaters and the rest. The brisk owner of a bucket-shop compared himself modestly to a mammoth, trampling down other mammoths in the primeval jungle. The business man destroyed other business men, under the extraordinary delusion that the eohippic horse had devoured other eohippic horses. The rich man suddenly discovered that it was not only convenient but cosmic to starve or pillage the poor, because pterodactyls may have used their little hands to tear each other's eyes. Science, that nameless being, declared that the weakest must go to the wall; especially in Wall Street. There was a rapid decline and degradation in the sense of responsibility in the rich, from the merely rationalistic eighteenth century to the purely scientific nineteenth. The great

Jefferson,[43] when he reluctantly legalised slavery, said he trembled for his country, knowing that God is just. The profiteer of later times, when he legalised usury or financial trickery, was satisfied with himself; knowing that Nature is unjust.

But, however that may be (and of course the moral malady has survived scientific mistake) the people who talked thus of cannibal horses and competitive oysters, did not understand what Darwin's thesis was. If later biologists have condemned it, it should not be condemned without being understood, widely as it has been accepted without being understood. The point of Darwinism was not that a bird with a longer beak (let us say) thrust it into other birds, and had the advantage of a duellist with a longer sword. The point of Darwinism was that the bird with the longer beak could reach worms (let us say) at the bottom of a deeper hole; that the birds who could not do so would die; and he alone would remain to found a race of long-beaked birds. Darwinism suggested that if this happened a vast number of times, in a vast series of ages, it might account for the difference between the beaks of a sparrow and a stork. But the point was that the fittest did not need to *struggle* against the unfit. The survivor had nothing to do except to survive, when the others could not survive. He survived because he alone had the features and organs necessary for survival. And, whatever be the truth about mammoths or monkeys, that is the exact truth about the present survival of religion. It is surviving because nothing else can survive.

Religion has returned; because all the various forms of scepticism that tried to take its place, and do its work, have by this time tied themselves into such knots that they cannot do anything. That chain of causation of which they were fond of talking seems really to have served them after the fashion of the proverbial rope; and when modern discussion gave them rope enough, they quite rapidly hanged themselves. For there is not a single one of the fashionable forms of scientific scepticism, or determinism, that does not end in stark paralysis, touching the practical conduct of human life. Take any three of the normal and necessary ideas on which civilisation and even society

---

[43] This reference is to a passage in Jefferson's *Notes on the State of Virginia*. Jefferson did not "legalize" slavery in Virginia; it had never been illegal.

depend. First, let us say, a scientific man of the old normal nineteenth-century sort would remark, "We can at least have common sense, in its proper meaning of a sense of reality common to all; we can have common morals, for without them we cannot even have a community; a man must in the ordinary sense obey the law; and especially the moral law." Then the newer sceptic, who is progressive and has gone further and fared worse, will immediately say, "Why should you worship the taboo of your particular tribe? Why should you accept prejudices that are the product of a blind herd instinct? Why is there any authority in the unanimity of a flock of frightened sheep?" Suppose the normal man falls back on the deeper argument: "I am not terrorised by the tribe; I do keep my independent judgment; I have a conscience and a light of justice within, which judges the world." And the stronger sceptic will answer: "If the light in your body be darkness—and it is darkness because it is only in your body—what are your judgments but the incurable twist and bias of your particular heredity and accidental environment? What can we know about judgments, except that they must all be equally unjust? For they are all equally conditioned by defects and individual ignorances, all of them different and none of them distinguishable; for there exists no single man so sane and separate as to be able to distinguish them justly. Why should your conscience be any more reliable than your rotting teeth or your quite special defect of eyesight? God bless us all, one would think you believed in God!" Then perhaps the normal person will get annoyed and say rather snappishly, "At least I suppose we are men of science; there is science to appeal to and she will always answer; the evidential and experimental discovery of real things." And the other sceptic will answer, if he has any sense of humour: "Why certainly. Sir Arthur Eddington[44] is Science; and he will tell you that science cannot destroy religion, or even defend the multiplication table. Sir Bertram Windle[45] was Science; and he would tell you that the scientific mind is completely satisfied in the Roman Catholic Church. For that matter, Sir Oliver

[44] See footnote 32, page 49, above.
[45] Bertram Windle (1858–1929) was an English Catholic anthropologist and physician who sought in his writings to demonstrate that there was no conflict between science and Church teachings.

Lodge[46] was Science; and he reached by purely experimental and evidential methods to a solid belief in ghosts. But I admit that there are men of science who cannot get to a solid belief in anything; even in science; even in themselves. There is the crystalographer of Cambridge who writes in the *Spectator* the lucid sentence: 'We know that most of what we know is probably untrue.' Does that help you on a bit, in founding your sane and solid society?"

We have of course seen just lately the most dramatic exit of great material scientists from the camp of Materialism. It was Eddington I think, who used the phrase that the universe seems to be more like a great thought than a great machine: and Dr. Whitney[47] as reported, has declared that there is no rational description of the ultimate cosmic motion except the Will of God. But it is the perishing of the other things, at least as much as the persistence of the one thing, that has left us at last face to face with the ancient religion of our fathers. The thing once called free thought has come finally to threaten everything that is free. It denies personal freedom in denying free will and the human power of choice. It threatens civic freedom with a plague of hygienic and psychological quackeries; spreading over the land such a network of pseudo-scientific nonsense as free citizens have never yet endured in history. It is quite likely to reverse religious freedom, in the name of some barbarous nostrum or other, such as constitutes the crude and ill-cultured creed of Russia. It is perfectly capable of imposing silence and impotence from without. But there is no doubt whatever that it imposes silence and impotence from within. The whole trend of it, which began as a drive and has ended in a drift, is towards some form of the theory that a man cannot help himself; that a man cannot mend himself; above all, that a man cannot free himself. In all its novels and most of its newspaper articles it takes for granted that men are stamped and fixed in certain types of abnormality of anarchical weakness; that

[46] Sir Oliver Lodge (1851–1940) was an English physicist who attempted to reconcile science and religion.

[47] Chesterton could be referring to Mary Watson Whitney (1847–1920), an American astronomer who published observations on the positions of comets and asteroids and on variable stars.

they are pinned and labelled in a museum of morality or immorality; or of that sort of unmorality which is more priggish than the
one and more hoggish than the other. We are practically told that
we might as well ask a fossil to reform itself. We are told that we are
asking a stuffed bird to repent. We are all dead, and the only comfort is that we are all classified. For by this philosophy, which is the
same as that of the blackest of Puritan heresies, we all died before
we were born. But as it is Kismet without Allah, so also it is Calvinism without God.

The agnostics will be gratified to learn that it is entirely due to
their own energy and enterprise, to their own activity in pursuing
their own antics, that the world has at last tired of their antics and
told them so. We have done very little against them; *non nobis, Domine*;[48] the glory of their final overthrow is all their own. We have
done far less than we should have done, to explain all that balance
of subtlety and sanity which is meant by a Christian civilisation.
Our thanks are due to those who have so generously helped us by
giving a glimpse of what might be meant by a Pagan civilisation.
And what is lost in that society is not so much religion as reason;
the ordinary common daylight of intellectual instinct that has guided
the children of men. A world in which men know that most of
what they know is probably untrue cannot be dignified with the
name of a sceptical world; it is simply an impotent and abject world,
not attacking anything, but accepting everything while trusting nothing; accepting even its own incapacity to attack; accepting its own
lack of authority to accept; doubting its very right to doubt. We are
grateful for this public experiment and demonstration; it has taught
us much. We did not believe that rationalists were so utterly mad
until they made it quite clear to us. We did not ourselves think that
the mere denial of our dogmas could end in such dehumanised and
demented anarchy. It might have taken the world a long time to
understand that what it had been taught to dismiss as mediaeval
theology was often mere common sense; although the very term

[48] *Non nobis, Domine* is Latin for "Not to us, O Lord" but to Thy name be the
glory, from Psalms.

common sense, or *communis sententia*, was a mediaeval conception. But it took the world very little time to understand that the talk on the other side was most uncommon nonsense. It was nonsense that could not be made the basis of any common system, such as has been founded upon common sense.

To take one example out of many; the whole question of Marriage has been turned into a question of Mood. The enemies of marriage did not have the patience to remain in their relatively strong position; that marriage could not be proved to be sacramental, and that some exceptions must be treated as exceptions, so long as it was merely social. They could not be content to say that it is not a sacrament but a contract, and that exceptional legal action might break a contract. They brought objections against it that would be quite as facile and quite as futile, if brought against any other contract. They said that a man is never in the same mood for ten minutes together; that he must not be asked to admire in a red daybreak what he admired in a yellow sunset; that no man can say he will even be the same man by the next month or the next minute; that new and nameless tortures may afflict him if his wife wears a different hat; or that he may plunge her into hell by putting on a pair of socks that does not harmonise with somebody else's carpet. It is quite obvious that this sort of sensitive insanity applies as much to any other human relation as to this relation. A man cannot choose a profession; because, long before he has qualified as an architect, he may have mystically changed into an aviator, or be convulsed in rapid succession by the emotions of a ticket-collector, a trombone-player and a professional harpooner of whales. A man dare not buy a house for fear a fatal stranger with the wrong sort of socks should come into it; or for fear his own mind should be utterly changed in the matter of carpets or cornices. A man may suddenly decline to do any business with his own business partner; because he also, like the cruel husband, wears the wrong necktie. And I saw a serious printed appeal for sympathy for a wife, who deserted her family because her psychology was incompatible with an orange necktie. This is only one application, as I say; but it exactly illustrates how the sceptical principle is now applied; and how scepticism has recently changed from apparent sense to quite self-evident nonsense. The heresies not only decay but destroy themselves; in any case they perish without a blow.

For the reply, not merely of religion but of reason and the rooted sanity of mankind, is obvious enough. "If you feel like that, why certainly you will not found families; or found anything else. You will not build houses; you will not make partnerships; you will not in any fashion do the business of the world. You will never plant a tree, lest you wish next week you had planted it somewhere else; you will never put a potato into a pot or stew, because it will be too late to take it out again; your whole mood is stricken and riddled with cowardice and sterility; your whole way of attacking any problem is to think of excuses for not attacking it at all. Very well; so be it; the Lord be with you. You may be respected for being sincere; you may be pitied for being sensitive; you may retain some of the corrective qualities which make it useful on occasion to be sceptical. But if you are too sceptical to do these things, you must stand out of the way of those who can do them; you must hand over the world to those who believe that the world is workable; to those who believe that men can make houses, make partnerships, make appointments, make promises—and keep them. And if it is necessary in order to keep a promise or boil a potato or behave like a human being, to believe in God making Man, in God being made Man, or in God made Man coming in the clouds in glory—well, then you must at least give a chance to these credulous fanatics who can believe the one and who can do the other." That is what I mean by the spiritual Survival of the Fittest. That is why the old phrase, which is probably a mistake in natural history, is a truth in supernatural history. The organic thing called religion has in fact the organs that take hold on life. It can feed where the fastidious doubter finds no food; it can reproduce where the solitary sceptic boasts of being barren. It may be accepting a miracle to believe in free will; but it is accepting madness, sooner or later, to disbelieve in it. It may be a wild risk to make a vow; but it is a quiet, crawling and inevitable ruin to refuse to make a vow. It may be incredible that one creed is the truth and the others are relatively false; but it is not only incredible, but also intolerable, that there is no truth either in or out of creeds, and all are equally false. For nobody can ever set anything right, if everybody is equally wrong. The intense interest of the moment is that the Man of Science, the hero of the modern world and the latest of the great servants of humanity, has suddenly and dramatically refused to have anything more to do with this dreary business of nibbling negation, and blind scratching and scraping away of the very foundations of the mastery of man. For the work of the sceptic for the past hundred years has indeed been very like the fruitless fury of some primeval monster; eyeless, mindless, merely destructive and devouring; a giant worm wasting away a world that he could not even see; a benighted and bestial life, unconscious of its own cause and of its own consequences. But Man has taken to himself again his own weapons; will and worship and reason and the vision of the plan in things; and we are once more in the morning of the world.

THE REACTION OF THE INTELLECTUALS

I have been asked if I think there is a reaction against the tendencies called "ultra-modern" and in favour of many things blasted by the term, "Victorian" and "virtuous" and "respectable," and other wild and wicked words. I answer that there is a reaction, and I am glad of it; but it is a reaction of a very peculiar kind. It is not what I expected. It is not even particularly what I wanted. But anything is a relief from the desolate dullness and staleness of the Bright Young Thing.

First, it will clear the human mind (and save the advanced mind from many disappointments) if we realise that there always *can* be a reaction, right or wrong, against anything, good or bad. Life is far too complex not to leave some desirable or defensible things behind with every movement it makes. We have reactions in favour of things much more remote than Victorianism. I always remember a confident and contemptuous phrase in one of Macaulay's[49] speeches for the Reform Bill, which abolished Rotten Boroughs.[50] "There has been no reaction. There will be no reaction. I no more expect a reaction in favour of Gatton and Old Sarum than a reaction in favour of Odin and Thor." I will not discuss whether there is a reaction in favour of Gatton and Old Sarum; there most certainly is a reaction against Reform Bills and Representative Government. But what amuses me is that, even while Macaulay said the words, there was beginning a most unmistakable reaction in favour of Odin and Thor. Carlyle already had pen in hand and his Northern genius was slowly turning into Nordic insanity. He was already telling us to go back to the stark Scandinavian beginnings. A little while afterwards Nietzsche took the next step by throwing over Christian ethics as well as theology, and invoking the old gods of violence and war. And it ended with a great German General (who had led through the Great

---

[49] Thomas Babington Macaulay (1800–1859) authored a multivolume history of England, and was Great Britain's most famous historian in the nineteenth century.

[50] The Reform Bill of 1832 broadened the franchise for parliamentary elections. Rotten boroughs were sparsely populated voting districts that held equal representation with more populous districts.

War and might have had enough of it) actually filling Germany with pagan propaganda and a publicity campaign in favour of Odin and Thor. So much for reactions in general. The most modern art finds the Ancient Greeks too modern and goes back to the Ancient Egyptians. We revive Primitive Art and may revive Prehistoric Art. We may paint on rock with red ochre, for all I know, or discover special qualities in stone hatchets and flint arrows.

There is a reaction; but that would not alone prove that the reaction is right. I think it is right; because it is a reaction in favour of civilisation; and against the destruction of civilisation. But with that word "civilisation" we come to the rather curious quality which this particular reaction shows. It is not, as I myself might have hoped or expected, a revolt of plain, old-fashioned people against the sophisticated. It is a revolt of the sophisticated. It is, at any rate, a revolt of the highly civilised; perhaps of the over-civilised. But if they are over-civilised, they are still highly intelligent. That is why they are kicking the Bright Young Thing down the street.

I will take one particular case which is rather a parable. Some time ago all the fine old English critics, Constant Readers and Conservative people generally, were in a ferment of fury and mockery against the impudent innovations of "the Sitwells";[51] that is, the three poets of that family. They were a proof that being modern means going mad. They were the very latest and loudest anarchists, destroying both rhyme and reason. I will not discuss their merits here. When Miss Sitwell accused the Dawn of "creaking," there were discussions as to her meaning. Her foes said it was random nonsense, like describing the sun as sneezing or the grass as blowing its nose. Her friends said it was a bold and novel way of suggesting something harsh and reluctant about the cold morning light. But everybody agreed that it was the very latest and newest experiment, whether in liberty or in lunacy. The Sitwells were accused of beating the big drum, or blowing their own trumpet; but it was agreed that their drums and trumpets were the newest musical instruments

---

[51] The Sitwells were Edith (1887–1964), Osbert (1892–1969) and Sacheverell (1897–1969).

of the queerest shape; and that they used the newest methods of shrieking for what they wanted. But what did they want?

Now, what the Sitwells want is Victorianism. What they do definitely desire, demand and incessantly describe, is a reaction to Victorian habits; to Victorian manners; and even to Victorian morals. As certainly as Shelley wanted a lot of wind and light and the rise of the pure pagan republic, as surely as Walt Whitman wanted democratic breadth and a sort of bodily brotherhood among men out-of-doors, so certainly what the Sitwells want is Victorian flower-beds and hothouses, Victorian coloured patchwork and curios under glass; and, in no small degree, Victorian etiquette, distance and dignity. This may be a fad but it is a fact; and it is a fact that vividly illustrates the real revolt against recent moral, or immoral, tendencies. The Victorian revolt is not a revolt of Victorians. It is a revolt of Post-Victorians or rather of Post-Post-Victorians. They are going back to something remote, as much as the Pre-Raphaelites[52] in going back to the Middle Ages. In both cases the reason is the same; because the modern ages have become too unbearably stupid for intelligent people. But the more modern case is the more acute case of this revolt against modernity among the moderns. To understand it, we must take a more general view of the singular situation in the world to-day.

Those specially called the Moderns, who are now most of them Ancients, conceived of human history as a progress in the sense of a procession. That is, they said that some slower people might bring up the rear but all were moving onward. They also supposed that certain bold sprits, whom they called the Pioneers of Progress, went on in front and made a path for mankind. I have a great admiration for Walt Whitman; but it cannot be denied that he did exclaim, in a moment of weakness, "Pioneers, O Pioneers!" It was characteristic of all that world; first, that it relied upon a metaphor; and second,

---

[52] The Pre-Raphaelite Brotherhood, a movement to infuse art with morality, flourished in mid-nineteenth-century England. Its members, most prominent of whom were William Holman Hunt, John Everett Millais and Dante Gabriel Rossetti, contended that the degeneration of Western art had begun in the Renaissance with Raphael.

that it got the metaphor quite wrong. Whitman seems to associate his intellectual pioneers with the practical pioneers of the American Civil War. But a pioneer is not a person who leads the army, or decides where it shall go. The pioneers in front are as much under orders as any camp-followers in the rear. If Sherman had thrown out pioneers to clear his road to Atlanta; and if the pioneers had seen a futuristic vision and gone off to found the future city of Oklahoma, Sherman would have been very much surprised; nay, vexed. And the moral is that the marching column of mankind must have some kind of notion of where it wants to go, before it can decide whether a pioneer is a useful pioneer or not.

Now, at this moment, the marching column of mankind is in an extraordinary position. For one thing, it is not marching. But it is marking time; because it still has the general notion that it ought to march. It may seem quaint to recur to Macaulay as well as Whitman; but it is better described in Macaulay's poem of Horatius than in Whitman's poem about the Pioneers; though to many, I fear, Whitman is now as distant as Macaulay. But it is really true that the exact and very extraordinary position of the procession at this moment is expressed with precision in the familiar lines:[53]

> "And those behind cried 'Forward!'
> And those before cried 'Back'!"

The camp-followers may be charging; but the pioneers are retreating. In other words, it is exactly the sort of bold and enquiring spirits, who were always said to be in advance of the age, who are now most doubtful about the desirability of advancing. It is exactly those who are content to follow tradition or convention or familiar fashions who are still following (as they suppose, at least) the tradition of progress, the convention of movement and the hundred fashions, familiar to the nineteenth-century, of appealing to the hope of change. Men are progressive because they are a little behind the times. They are reactionary because they are a little in advance of the times. It sounds like a paradox; but it is really a very practical and even

[53] The quotation is from Macaulay's *Lays of Ancient Rome* (1842).

inevitable state of things, given certain conditions. Those behind will still cry "Forward!"; and only those far in front will cry "Back!"; when the vanguard of the army has come suddenly to the edge of a precipice.

In short, I maintain that it is the Intellectuals (for want of a more intellectual term) who have now suddenly discovered the dangers of mere novelty, of mere anarchy, of mere negation. It is not all the Intellectuals, of course; and certainly not those who modestly gave themselves that name in the middle of the nineteenth-century. For these, by the ironic operation of their own favourite argument, are now old and venerable and established and respected; and, therefore, of no importance whatever. Men like Bertrand Russell, and H. G. Wells, are left behind by the advance; and are, therefore, under the illusion that it is still advancing. The particular state of mind I mean (which is not always a very pretty state of mind at present) is peculiar to a section of the younger Intellectuals. And, whatever it is, it is not a positive faith in the promise of the future or the tendencies of the present. If we take any typical contemporary poetry of the sort that is sensitive and critical, say the poems of Mr. Osbert Sitwell, it is quite obvious that they are *not* merely in revolt against the nineteenth-century; though the progressive theory was bound up with the nineteenth-century. They are in revolt against the twentieth-century; and potentially more in revolt against the twenty-first.

But the point is that it is because they are so very Modern that they have rebelled against Modernism. It is because they have themselves seen all the new tricks, and in many cases played all the new tricks, that they have realised before anybody else that the whole bag of tricks may soon be played out. Mr. Humbert Wolfe[54] may be justified in beginning every line with a small letter; indeed, in that he is classical rather than revolutionary; for the old Latin texts were always printed so. But he is far too intelligent a man not to see that those who would prove themselves progressive, by abandoning all capital letters, can only prove themselves still more progressive by abandoning all small letters; and that this sort of destructive reform

[54] Humbert Wolfe (1885–1940) was a popular British satiric poet and critic.

can only end in a blank page. So this kind of destructive progress
ends in a blank wall. Mr. Sitwell may think himself right, in this or
that case, in attaching a musical adjective to an entirely visual or
pictorial substantive. But he can see, as well as anybody else, that if
a hundred howling imitators come in and claim the right to attach
any adjective to any substantive, it is not so much a question of
literature being lawless as of its ceasing to be anything at all. And we
see more and more, every day, this curious sort of new alarm spreading among the most intelligent of the new schools; which is almost
unintelligible to many of the old schools; and especially to that very
old school which supposes that the young have no business to be
anything but reckless and revolutionary.

I will take the case of two of the most acute and individual
among contemporary writers, one probably younger than the other,
at least in fashion and fame; one American and the other English,
and the inheritor of a name already famous for a very English
style. I will take the cases of Mr. T. S. Eliot and Mr. Aldous Huxley. They are different enough, of course; but they exactly express
two different ways of recoiling from the recent riot and vulgarity
of the merely "modern" world. Mr. Eliot, who began like a child
of his age with the recognised stark and jagged experiments in free
verse, has come to have something like a suspicion of every sort of
freedom. He had come to stand for an almost cloistered refine-
ment, full of the virginal traditions of old religion and repudiating
not only the demagogy of to-day, but even the democracy of yes-
terday. There are passages in the works of Mr. Aldous Huxley which
few will call cloistered, which few, perhaps, will call virginal. But
he is none the less a representative of the same reaction against
recent vulgarity and vice. Only he reacts more in the manner of
Swift; showing the ugly their own ugliness; even pelting the filthy
with samples of their own filth. But he is, if not on the side of the
angels, at least horribly bored with the devils. Anyone who will
read his admirable account of Hollywood, which he calls, "The
City of Dreadful Joy," will find it more dreadful than joyful. There
is a fight against the recent licence; but what is fighting it is a sort
of fierce fastidiousness.

I am not imagining this reaction because I want it; for, indeed, it is not especially the reaction that I want. I should have hoped for a popular revolt against perversions and pedantries of vice, which have never, in fact, been popular. I should have liked the ordinary, old-fashioned, obstinate people, who still stick to the notion of some connection between themselves and their own babies, to rise and bash in the heads of the inhuman prigs whose ideal is a sort of prophetic infanticide. I should like a howling rabble of really respectable people (and the rabble is still really respectable) to burn down the houses where Luxury takes on its true Latin sense of Luxuria. I should like the normal people, who live on beef and beer, to make war on the hypocritical cranks who take their vegetarianism in the form of vegetable cocktails less wholesome than the fruit of the vine. I should prefer the Intellectuals to be slaughtered by what may be called the Morals; and the mob is still very moral. But the great point is that they should be slaughtered; if not by the clubs of the crowd, then by the rapier of the more intellectual Intellectual. God moves in a mysterious way and does not disdain the strangest or the humblest instruments; and we must not be ashamed of finding ourselves, if necessary, on the side of the cultivated and the clever.

Or again, it might have been that picturesque paradox; a revolt of the old against the young. It might have been a rebellion of oppressed parents breaking the yoke of servile obedience now laid on them by their tyrannical sons and daughters. It might have been the heavy father breaking out of the coal-cellar with the original big stick, or the maiden aunt emerging from the bedroom armed with the poker; and the joyous spectacle of their smashing the gramophones and the saxophones and the ukuleles, hurling away the cocktails, wrecking the racing cars and generally showing that there is life in the old dog yet. But, as a fact, it does not seem to be coming through the fury of the father or the grandfather but rather with the slowly maturing disgust of the great-grandson with the manifest idiocy of the grandson.

It is not coming by the big stick or the cudgels of the populace; but by something which I have compared to a rapier; and might compare to a razor. Some young men of the school of Mr. Aldous Huxley have, indeed, a touch of pessimism that is only too suggestive of a razor; at once the symbol of elegance and of suicide. And yet there is a broader sense in which this is, perhaps, rather too true. When the Victorians rebuked little boys for playing with razors or rapiers, or such acute instruments and arguments ensued, the elders often used a proverbial expression here very relevant: "If you get so sharp as that, you will cut yourself." The minority of the most intelligent, in the younger generation, has really become very sharp; and it has really discovered the peril of cutting itself. Men like Mr. Huxley and Mr. Eliot have the sense to see that the half-truths of the sceptic are not only edged tools, but double-edged tools. They cut the ground from under rationalism as well as from under religion; they can be used to wound democracy as easily as despotism; in the last resort they can inoculate the mind with doubts about doubt itself. More and more the really clever young man will find that he has grown sharp enough to cut himself; and, if he does not try something beyond scepticism, he will grow sceptical enough to cut his throat.

Lastly, why do I think this small minority of rather fastidious and over-refined persons will finally have an effect? I answer, with a profound sigh, because of the great social institution which we call Snobbery. As soon as the quite brainless mob of Bright Young Things discovers that it is really being *despised*, as a mob of dull old things (though it were only by two well-educated minor poets) there will be a panic. The mass of the immoralists never believed in immorality or in anything else. They never really thought that wrong was right, because they never really thought at all. They merely believed what they were told; that being lawless was the latest thing. If once they hear that there is something later still, even later than the latest, they will rush for it and roll in the mud in front of it, though it were a Hermit out of the desert like St. Anthony. If it is a humorous, but slightly superior young man, who regards all their vulgar and raucous games as *vieux jeu*, and will only condescend to talk about Humanism and St. Thomas Aquinas, they will grovel before him. I know them. They play the goat; but they none the less do it like sheep. For they are sheep that have not a shepherd, and the shepherd named Pan is dead.

LEVITY—OR LEVITATION

I do not see why a man should not sometimes have a holiday, even while he is doing his work, and write about something merely because it amuses him. I know I should be doing my duty as a Distributist, doing it dismally with the pen when others are already doing it more nobly with the plough. But, for once in a way, I am going to write merely for fun; and about something only because it is funny. And the funniest thing I can find for miles round is in a paper called *Psychic News*, a past issue of which was adorned with a portrait of me, accompanied with the extraordinary and rather mysterious caption, "G.K.C., the Catholic who goes up in the air." Believing as I do in miracles, I have never claimed levitation as a power particularly likely to be manifested in my own case. But though not at present drawn irresistibly towards levitation, I am much tempted to levity. The charges are rather vague, except that they all seem to be equally unfortunate in relation to the facts of the case. The writer seemed to take it for granted that an article quite plainly signed by somebody else must really have been written by me, and written by me from no other motive but a fanatical Catholicism, although the man who really wrote is not a Catholic at all and said nothing whatever to suggest in any way that he was. He, however, is supremely capable of looking after himself, and the mere facts about this absurd muddle I have dealt with elsewhere. At the moment I only wish to wallow in sheer shameless enjoyment of the way in which the *Psychic News* attacks the Catholic Church and attacks me. I admit that this is mere self-indulgence on my part. I know that numbers of judicious friends will tell me that I ought not to take any notice of such an article. But nothing that can be called human is uninteresting, and this involves, to begin with, one puzzle which always interests me very much. And that is why people who fly into a rage with the Catholic Church always use an extraordinary diction, or verbal style, in which all sorts of incommensurate things are jumbled up together, so that the very order of the words is a joke. "Spiritualism depends only on the evidence which people receive in their own

homes. It does not require priests. Neither do enquirers have to buy
rosaries or beads, or crucifixes, or pay for candles or masses." It
must be a dreadful moment of indecision for the enquirers, when
they have to make up their minds whether they will buy rosaries or
beads. But the last term is the best; and here the order of words is
especially significant. Apparently the first object of a Catholic is to
get a candle. If once he can get hold of a candle, and walk about
everywhere clasping his candle, he is all right. But if he cannot get
a candle, he has the alternative of purchasing a mass; an instrument
that is a sort of substitute for a candle.

Now I did not, as it happens, launch any grand persecuting personal spiritual attack on Spiritualism, as this writer imaginatively
described. But if I did, as of course I might, I do think I could
make a better job of attacking Spiritualism than he does of attacking
Catholicism. I should not talk as if a Spiritualist hung suspended
between the two divine dogmas of the Sacredness of Tambourines
and the Return of the Dead. I should not talk as if men chose between
a planchette and a Ouija-board. I should not talk about "tables or
furniture," or imply that a trumpet was the same sort of thing as a
séance. But I never read an attack on Catholicism without finding
this ignorant gabble of terms all topsy-turvy. There is always some
such medley of misused words, in which mitres, misereres, nones,
albs, croziers, virgins and viaticums tumble over each other without
the wildest hope that anybody could possibly know what any of
them mean. That is the first curiosity about this kind of writing.
We can now go back to the only sentence in the paragraph in which
anything like a meaning is apparent. It is that passage in which, we
are told, Spiritualism does without a priesthood.

It does not require priests. It only requires a spiritual aristocracy
really much more exclusive and privileged than priests; seeing they
have direct access to new revelations, and their superiority is in their
personal spiritual structure; they are abnormal as priests are not necessarily abnormal. But, however that may be, the paper in question
reveals some remarkable impressions about spiritual functions and
degrees. There is an astonishing caption under a picture of St. Joan
of Arc; saying that she did not care whether she was a saint or a

witch, because "she had a job to do and did it." How refreshing this language is. How full of the fifteenth century! Joan was just all out to get that job. She reckoned she could hold down that job. Gee! Joan wasn't the sort of skirt to bother about whether it came from God or the Devil, when there was a good job to hold down. The paper informs us that its religion is entirely founded on facts; but it seems possible to manufacture a good deal of abstract vulgarity without employing them. It were vain, I suppose, to point out the historical fact that Joan debated desperately for days and days to prove she was not a witch, long after it was obvious that her job, as a job, was either done or done for. But might not the suggestion, that it does not matter whether one is a witch or a saint, explain something of the distrust that some of us feel about Spiritualism?

As I am writing this for fun, I would not say very much about the central mystery of my own religion, or the laboriously offensive terms in which the writer asks me to "prove" Transubstantiation, as he apparently claims to "prove" Spiritualism. To him I am content to say one thing. Suppose the Church had tried to give such proofs, and with such results. Suppose Pope after Pope, and Priest after Priest, had stood up at the altar rails promising on the spot to prove Transubstantiation. And suppose Pope after Pope, and Priest after Priest, had been exposed as proving it by a faked apparatus in the Communion Table, by hidden wires in the cross and candles, and all the apparatus of fraud. Suppose, while many priests were doubtless honest men and perhaps honest dupes, it was a plain, palpable historical fact that the miracle had again and again been a mere conjuring trick, and the most famous Catholic saints had been caught and exposed doing the trick. If *that* had happened, I venture to say that the Eucharistic Congress would not now be so much respected by the whole civilised world; or by everybody except the hooligans of Portadown[55] and journalists of the *Psychic News*.

---

[55] Portadown is a municipal borough in northern Ireland known for its linen and cotton goods industry.

THE CASE FOR HERMITS

Anyone who has ever protected a little boy from being bullied at school, or a little girl from some childish persecution at a party, or any natural person from any minor nuisance, knows that the being thus badgered tends to cry out, in a simple but singular English idiom, "Let me alone!" It is seldom that the child of nature breaks into the cry, "Let me enjoy the fraternal solidarity of a more socially organised group-life." It is rare even for the protest to leap to the lips in the form, "Let me run around with some crowd that has got dough enough to hit the high spots." Not one of these positive modern ideals presents itself to that untutored mind; but only the ideal of being "let alone." It is rather interesting that so spontaneous, instinctive, almost animal an ejaculation contains the word *alone*.

There are now a great many boys and girls, both old and young, who are really in that state of mind; not only through being teased, but also through being petted. Most of them will fiercely deny it, since it contradicts the conventions of their new generation; just as a child kept up too late at night will more and more indignantly deny the desire to go to bed. Indeed I am always expecting to hear that a scientific campaign has been opened against Sleep. Sooner or later the Prohibitionists will turn their attention to the old tribal traditional superstition of Sleep; and they will say that the sluggard is merely encouraged by the cowardice of the moderate sleeper. There will be tables of statistics, showing how many hours of output are lost by miners, smelters, plumbers, plasterers, and every trade in which (it will be noted) men have contracted the habit of sleep; tables showing the shortage of aconite, alum, apples, beef, beetroot, bootlaces, etc., and other statistics carefully demonstrating that work of this kind can only rarely be performed by sleep-walkers. There will be all the scientific facts, except one scientific fact. And that is the fact that if men do not have Sleep, they go mad. It is also a fact that if men do not have Solitude, they go mad. You can see that, by the way they go on, when the poor miserable devils only have Society.

The incident of Miss Fitzpatrick, the lady who really liked to be alone, challenges all recent fashions, which are all for Society without Solitude. We must Get Together; as the gunman said when he ran his machine-gun into two other machine-guns and killed all the children caught between them. And we know that this sociability and communal organisation has already produced in fashionable society all that sweetness and light, all that courtesy and charity, all that True Christianity of pardon and patience, which we see in the modern organisers of gangs or "group-life." In contrast with this happy mood now pervading our literature and conversation, it is customary to point to hermits and solitaries as if they were savages and man-haters.

But it is not true. It is not true in history or human fact. The line that ran, "Turn, gentle hermit of the Vale," was truer to the real tradition about the real hermits. They were doubtless, from a modern standpoint, lunatics; but they were nice lunatics. Twenty touches could illustrate what I mean; for instance, the fact that they could make pets of the wild aminals that came naturally to them. But many of them really had charity—even to human beings. They felt more kindly about men than men in the Forum or the Mart felt about each other. Doubtless there have been merely sulky solitaries; unquestionably there have been sham cynics and *cabotins*,[56] like Diogenes. But he and his sort are very careful not to be *really* solitary; careful to hang about the market-place like any demagogue. Diogenes was a tub-thumper, as well as a tub-dweller. And that sort of professional sulks remains; but it is sulks without solitude. We all know there are geniuses, who must go out into polite society in order to be impolite. We all know there are hostesses who collect lions and find they have got bears. I fear there was a touch of that in the social legend of Thomas Carlyle and perhaps of Tennyson. But these men must have a society in which to be unsociable. The hermits, especially the saints, had a solitude in which to be sociable.

St. Jerome lived with a real lion; a good way to avoid being lionised. But he was very sociable with the lion. In his time, as in ours,

---

[56] *Cabotins* is French for "bad actors".

sociability of the conventional sort had become social suffocation. In the decline of the Roman Empire, people got together in amphitheatres and public festivals, just as they now get together in trams and tubes. And there were the same feelings of mutual love and tenderness, between two men trying to get a seat in the Colosseum, as there are now between two men trying to get the one remaining seat on a Tooting tram. Consequently, in that last Roman phase, all the most amiable people rushed away into the desert, to find what is called a hermitage; but might almost be called a holiday. The man was a hermit because he was more of a human being; not less. It was not merely that he felt he could get on better with a lion than with the sort of men who would throw him to the lions. It was also that he actually liked men better when they let him alone. Now nobody expects anybody, except a very exceptional person, to become a complete solitary. But there is a strong case for more Solitude; especially now that there is really no Solitude.

The reason why even the normal human being should be half a hermit is that it is the only way in which his mind can have a half-holiday. It is the only way to get any fun even out of the facts of life; yes, even if the facts are games and dances and operas. It bears most resemblance to the unpacking of luggage. It has been said that we live on a railway station; many of us live in a luggage van; or wander about the world with luggage that we never unpack at all. For the best things that happen to us are those we get out of what has already happened. If men were honest with themselves, they would agree that actual social engagements, even with those they love, often seem strange brief, breathless, thwarted or inconclusive. Mere society is a way of turning friends into acquaintances. The real profit is not in meeting our friends, but in having met them. Now when people merely plunge from crush to crush, and from crowd to crowd, they never discover the positive joy of life. They are like men always hungry, because their food never digests; also, like those men, they are cross. There is surely something the matter with modern life when all the literature of the young is so cross. That is something of the secret of the saints who went into the desert. It is in society that men quarrel with their friends; it is in solitude that they forgive them. And before the society-man criticises the saint, let him remember that the man in the desert often had a soul that was like a honey-pot of human kindness, though no man came near to taste it; and the man in the modern salon, in his intellectual hospitality, generally serves out wormwood for wine.

In conclusion, I will take one very modern and even topical case. I do not believe in Communism, certainly not in compulsory Communism. And it is typical of this acrid age that what we all discuss is compulsory Communism. I often sympathise with Communists, which is quite a different thing; but even these I respect rather as bold or honest or logical than as particularly genial or kindly. Nobody will claim that modern Communism is a specially sweet-tempered or amiable thing. But if you will look up the legends of the earliest Hermits, you will find a very charming anecdote, about two monks who really were Communists. And one of them tried to explain to the other how it was that quarrels arose about private property. So he thumped down a stone and observed theatrically, "This stone is mine." The other, slightly wondering at his taste, said, "All right; take it." Then the teacher of economics became quite vexed and said, "No, no; you mustn't say that. You must say it is yours; and then we can fight." So the second hermit said it was his; whereupon the first hermit mechanically gave it up; and the whole lesson in Business Methods seems to have broken down. Now you may agree or disagree with the Communist ideal, of cutting oneself off from commerce, which those two ascetics followed. But is there not something to suggest that they were rather nicer people than the Communists we now meet in Society? Somehow as if Solitude improved the temper?

KILLING THE NERVE

It is now generally agreed, with great cheerfulness and good temper, that one of the chief features of the state of Peace we now enjoy is the killing of a considerable number of harmless human beings. We are not wild and reckless and pugnacious in such things, even as these Latins. Relatively, we seem almost reconciled to the general notion of killing; so long as we can feel a real assurance that it is aimless and purposeless and fruitless. If an old woman is knocked down dead in the quiet village street where she played as a child, if a gutter-boy is not quite quick enough in getting out of the gutter and suffers the death penalty for his negligence, we all agree that it is very regrettable. But it does not withdraw the attention of some of us from quite exclusive concentration upon the horrors of war, because nobody could confuse an old woman crossing the road with an old-world romance in any way connected with adventure or valour; and the boy has not ventured into the road (thank God) under any delusion that he is sacrificing himself for his native land. If death strikes down suddenly somebody who does not expect to die, and is not deceived by any nonsense about being faithful unto death ... O death, where is thy sting? If a tramp is taken to a pauper's grave unstained by any hopes or dreams of war or revolution, or any vision of justice victorious ... O grave, where is thy victory? It is obvious that death is a very different thing when it is the product of such peaceful surroundings. The modern version of Killing No Murder is that only militarism is murder; and there is nothing wrong with killing when it is not military.

But I have here introduced the word killing in a lighter sense; even lighter than that in which some progressives take the killing in the streets. For there are other things, though they are things less vivid and less sacred, which are killed in the streets. Even as it is we use the world "kill" in a more metaphorical sense. For instance, we talk of colours killing each other. And, as one example out of many, it may be noted that we do live in a scheme of social life in which colours kill each other. That is, we live in a world which gives us a vast exhibition of that vividness which is symbolised by colour, but which is wholly without that concerted unity of rule or tradition which is symbolised by harmony in colour. The illuminated advertisements of a big city like London, which is now in this respect almost indistinguishable from New York, exhibit exactly that contradiction between colour and design. The design, even in the sense of the purpose, is patchy and personal and not only vulgar but essentially venal. The colour is often the best and most beautiful experience given to the senses of man, if only man were in a position to make the best of it. The psychological effect produced by random commercial illumination is something which is to the real possibilities of colour what a drunken slumber is to the divine gift of wine. Or rather, it should be compared to that habit, which springs up so easily in Prohibitionist or semi-Prohibitionist countries, of trying to get the best out of the divine gift of wine by preceding it with excessive quantities of whisky, following it by equally excessive quantities of beer, or possibly beginning the whole banquet with liqueurs and ending it with cocktails. In short, Prohibitionists get drunk because they have never been taught to drink; and commercial advertising wastes its artistic materials, even when it possesses them, because it has never been taught to colour or even to enjoy colours. Colours are being killed; and they are being killed by being worked to death. The nerve is being killed; and it is being killed by being overstimulated and therefore stunted and stunned.

When I was a child, I had a toy-theatre, illuminated in those days by candles (to which perhaps the psychoanalyst will trace my subsequent downfall into ecclesiastical crypts and cloisters) and in the ordinary way I was quite content with this type of illumination, the candles seeming to my barbarous mind to be themselves like a forest of fairy trees, with flames for flowers. There were also yet more rich and rare delights, which were sufficiently rare to those not sufficiently rich. It was sometimes possible to purchase a sort of dark red powder, which when ignited burst into a rich red light. Fire was wonderful enough—but red fire! But then I was only a dull Victorian infant somewhere between five and seven; and I only used red fire rarely; when it was effective. Living under such limitations, my immature brain perceived that it was more suitable to some things than to others; as, for instance, to a goblin coming up through a trap-door out of the cavern of the King of the Copper Mines, or to the final conflagration that made a crimson halo round the dark mill and castle of the execrable Mad Miller. I should not even then have used red fire in a scene showing the shepherd (doubtless a prince in disguise) piping to his lambs in the pale green meadows of spring; or in a scene in which glassy gauzes of green and blue waved in the manner of waves round the cold weeds and fishes at the entrance to Davy Jones's Locker. Science and progress and practical education and knowledge of the world are necessary before people can make blunders like that. Therefore, that red fire of the nursery still glows in my memory as in inward imaginative revelation, in spite of years, in spite of time, in spite even of passing through the streets of modern London.

In the London streets to-day, in what Mr. Cuthbert Baines has so vividly called, "the floodlit, bloodlit street," the rare effect of red fire is wholly wasted and ruined, by the loss of its rarity and by the loss of its suitability. The child who has been made too familiar with all that redhot lettering will probably never have the romance that I remember in my childhood; and it is perhaps strictly true to say that he will never see red fire in his life. First, of course, because he has seen too much of it. For this is not the decorative process of using red in a scheme of colour; it is simply the dull process of painting the town red. But second, also, because the toy-theatre showed him little pictures of large things; and the town signs show him large pictures of little things. He will very soon discover that the ideas associated with these signs, the motives of the men who put them up, the mood of the men who accept them, are things connected entirely with dreary money-grubbing or shoddy luxury. He will be unable to get any great vista or vision out of a glimpse; he will know nothing but a glaring wilderness of proclamations that have emphasis without significance; and will grow up without any poetical associations with a colour he has only seen used to sell a cosmetic or a quack medicine.

THE CASE OF CLAUDEL

I have heard a story, which I have never verified either by history or topography, otherwise known as being on the spot, to the effect that the French Academy accepted the accident of the absence of Molière from its records with a magnificent gesture. It may have been only a tradition about something that somebody planned to do; it may even have been only a tale of somebody about what ought to be done; but it is exactly the sort of tradition that would represent the nation; and it is exactly the sort of thing that Frenchmen would or could have done. The French Academy, founded by Richelieu for the establishment of classical literature in the country, naturally passed over a wandering play-actor and playwright like Molière; just as Oxford and Cambridge would have passed over a wandering play-actor and playwright like Shakespeare. But here the story, even if it is only a story, stikes the note that only the French can strike. For it was said that the French Academy erected in its inner courts a special statue of Molière, with the inscription "Rien ne manque à sa gloire; il manque à la nôtre" [57] ... and if you want to know what is the difference between the atmosphere of France and England, both of them very jolly atmospheres in their way, you have only to imagine anybody making, or even anybody suggesting, a public apology of that sort to Shakespeare. Can you imagine a huge statue of Shakespeare in Balliol Quad, inscribed with the statement, "Shakespeare never went to Balliol." Can you conceive even Cambridge rearing a colossal monument to Dickens, to celebrate the fact that he never had a University education—or indeed any other education? If that story about Molière is true, or even if it is a true parable or fable, there is an obvious moral to the fable. The English rather ignore defeats; the French rather exaggerate defeats; but the French do sometimes have the talent of snatching victories out of defeats.

[57] Chesterton's translation of this French quotation is: "Nothing is wanting to his glory; but he is wanting to ours."

A little while ago, to my great regret, the French Academy suffered a very serious defeat. It was when it preferred a clever writer of rather decadent verse to Paul Claudel;[58] but nobody supposes, I hope, that it was M. Claudel who was defeated. If we are to talk about anybody really great being defeated, let us say that Richelieu was defeated. A man of the first rank of French Letters, which the great Cardinal loved, and the Catholic culture which he also loved, with all his diplomatic and even unscrupulous encouragement of those who hated it, has been met with a sort of mute resistance; presumably by those who hated more than the most unscrupulous Cardinal could ever do. Without presuming to pronounce upon the literary comparison, it is enough to say that even if the Academy were right, it would here prove itself entirely academic. It would be proved in the fact that nobody in the literary world has heard of Claudel's rival; and everybody in the literary world has heard of Claudel. He is recognised as standing for something quite literally from China to Peru; at least from Japan to Washington. It looks as if the Academy has made one of its rather rare mistakes; and without the obvious excuses which applied to the case of Molière. And it looks as if there might some day be another statue, with another inscription: "Nothing is wanting to his glory; but he is wanting to ours."

There is no space here even to suggest the sumptuous wealth of images and ideas in the work of Paul Claudel. It is only important to note the fact, as a fact of history rather than of literature, that it is on his side, and not on the other side, that the wealth of ideas can now be found. It might very well happen, at one time it probably did happen, that the historic culture he represents had dwindled down to narrow channels and rare and isolated notes; like the last pipe of the pastoral poets that sounded from the eighteenth-century clerics imitating the innocence of the Georgics;[59] or that Irish harp of which a single string snapped whenever a heart had broken for liberty. But to-day it is exactly the other way. It is the rationalistic tradition of the nineteenth century that has narrowed into monotony and

---

[58] Paul Claudel (1868–1955) was a French Catholic poet, playwright and diplomat.

[59] The *Georgics* is Virgil's long poem on agriculture, beekeeping and livestock-raising.

repetition. It is the artist who is an atheist who has taken refuge in a garden, to escape from the cry of all the ancient Christian civilization for the ploughing of all the fields of the earth. It is the musical instrument of the modernist that has broken all its strings but one, like the lute in the agnostic picture of Hope; and continues to strike the same few chords of truth remaining to it, but drearily and all on one note. Nobody denies, and certainly I do not deny, that the truths of the emancipated epoch are still true, even when thus isolated and irrelevant; just as the spiritual truths were still true, even when repeated mechanically by the court chaplains or stale preachers of the eighteenth century. But in the matter of fullness, of richness, and of variety, the whole advantage is now with the ancient cause. The thoughts that throng in a sort of hubbub, in a work like *The Satin Slipper,*[60] are like a crowd of living men bursting the barriers of a deserted fortress. It is Claudel or the same type of man who is now storming the Bastille; a prison with all the harshness and inhumanity of a prison, except that it now contains fewer and fewer prisoners. An empty prison may be almost more depressing than a full prison; and such an empty prison is the tradition of academic scepticism to-day. Prejudice, the very spirit of a prison, alone shuts out the new generation from the full realization of the greater fruitfulness promised by the revival of Christendom. In one sense we may agree with all the old and weary jounalists who say that the age is to be the age of Youth; but its most youthful manifestation is in something that renews its youth like the eagle.

[60] *The Satin Slipper* is a play written by Claudel in the 1920s and set in the sixteenth century.

THE HIGHER NIHILISM

Mr. Middleton Murry[61] has written a generous, a stimulating and rather a strange book. It is called *The Necessity of Communism*: and my own first feelings about it may be expressed by saying that I have much more sympathy with the Communism than with the Necessity. I cannot but feel that Mr. Middleton Murry is caught in a sort of net of necessity; that his spirited and active mind is actually hampered by his queer religion of destiny. The reader trips over it, as if it were barbed wire, when striding through what is otherwise an open field of freedom and fairmindedness. To take one example; no Catholic could possibly ask for a more just or even generous judgment on the Middle Ages, and their relation to the Reformation, than that given in Mr. Murry's chapter called "The Pattern of History"; and yet it ends with a twist of phrase so abrupt and perverse that I almost cried out aloud at the inconsequence. "In England the Church was expropriated, by men who had not as individuals the faintest ethical superiority over those they expropriated, but who had the impersonal justification of being instruments of economic destiny." Now, with all respect, I do not know in the least what the last words of that sentence mean. What is "impersonal justification"? How can anything except a person be justified, and how can he be justified except by another person judging him to be just? What are "instruments of economic destiny" or any other destiny? Instruments mean tools chosen by some person for some purpose. Who is Destiny; and in what sense can he have a purpose? It always seems to me that all this sort of thing is not even metaphysics, far less metabiology, but simply metaphor. It is all the more difficult to deal with, because the ideas for which it stands are delivered quite dogmatically as dogmas. Mr. Middleton Murry tells us at the very beginning that a man must be a complete materialist; that it is mere shilly-shallying to be only a behaviourist. But he does not give a man like me any reason for being either; and I have not the smallest

<hr>

[61] John Middleton Murry (1889–1957) was an English literary critic and editor.

intention of being either. He says that any reversion to the past is "forbidden," and I can only say "By whom?" It would be a mere wanton veto on all art and action to forbid us to take materials from the past. But as a fact it is impossible for anybody to avoid using the past. In reality, it is impossible to use anything except the past. And why is it any more forbidden to me to say that the Catholic Church is a thing of the future and the present, as well as the past, than it is to Mr. Murry to say that Karl Marx fulfilled the purpose of the Hebrew Prophets or that Jesus of Nazareth became the supreme type of disinterestedness? But in logic there is no need even to go back to Jesus or the Jewish prophets. Karl Marx is as much a part of the past as King John Sobieski;[62] and the Russian Revolution is as past as the Roman Empire. The book is full of violent affirmations of this sort, entirely unsupported by arguments of any sort. Nevertheless, there is an argument running through the book; and a very curious and interesting one it is.

The writer starts, as he starts with so many unexplained things, with the very dangerous word, "disinterested." It is dangerous because a mere touch will make it mean "uninterested"; in the sense of the Buddhist and the pessimist. We all know it has a sane sense, as meaning sincerely unselfish, self-sacrificing for a faith, and so on. But Mr. Murry does not mean merely giving up our pleasures for the sake of our ideals. In some places, he really seems to mean giving up our ideals, or some of our ideals, for a sort of super-ideal which has sometimes precious little to say for itself, except that it is Destiny. There really is a wild cry from Asia in his classic speech; an altruism that is almost nihilism; a sacrifice that is nearly suicide. We are to give up liberty; we are to give up everything. This passionate paradox is undoubtedly sincere; and yet it conceals another paradox which it will be well to watch and suspect. Morally, it is all very heroic; but intellectually, it actually contains too much caution; it is more cautious than wise. It has behind its position two alternative lines of retreat. For the logical reader will at once perceive that, by

---

[62] King John III Sobieski ruled Poland from 1674 to 1696 and was a key figure in driving the Turks from the gates of Vienna in 1683.

thus rising into wild renunciation, the controversialist really has it both ways. Wherever Communism can be made attractive, he will make it attractive. Wherever Communism is quite obviously repulsive, he will say it proves the selfless hardihood of Communists who embrace so repulsive a thing. When it is human, it is in sympathy with all humanity; when it is inhuman, it calls for a superhuman sympathy. When it is good it is good; and when it is bad, they are very good to swallow it. This form of Necessity might be found in that proverb from the mouldering past: "Heads I win, tails you lose."

What Mr. Middleton Murry wants, of course, is real religion; and in parts of this book he seems to be growing desperate, or almost going mad, under the limitations of his unreal religion. He has got authority in the wrong place and asceticism in the wrong place. He is more limited by the idea of Destiny than we are by the idea of Deity. And he wants man to sacrifice civilisation as monks sacrifice luxury. He seems almost satisfied with it as a giant gesture of renunciation; there is really uncommonly little in this book about what will be the practical advantages of Communism when established. Reading between the lines, we almost find the meaning to be merely this: that he and the rest of us have come to breaking point; and this is the obvious point at which to break. There are other aspects of the book, with many of which I warmly agree, but I will conclude by saying that my fundamental objection to his Communism is that it consents to be the heir of Capitalism. His unfortunate necessitarianism narrows the possibilities of politics; and is content to say that industrialism has turned the world into One Man, who is aching in all his limbs. No doubt; and so would you and I, if we were all unnaturally tied to each other neck and heels, that we might make up together the monstrous and tottering figure of a pantomime ogre. But I do not want the ogre; I only want to cut him up. I am more revolutionary than Mr. Middleton Murry. I do not believe the unnatural monster will ache any the less, because he calls himself a Communist. I am more sceptical than Mr. Middleton Murry. I deny the pantomime myth of the One Man; and I should like to break him up again into men.

THE ASCETIC AT LARGE

My note on the Communism of Mr. Middleton Murry reads to me as rather too hasty and hostile; because I had no space to mention some strong and substantial parts of the book; notably those expressing contempt for the respectable sort of Socialist who will not call himself a Communist. The study of 'parasitic' Parliamentary Labour is masterly, and my own sympathies would be all with a man like Mr. Maxton as compared with a man like Mr. Thomas.[63] But the sequel is still puzzling; for in the last short note there is no practical programme except a Minimum Wage for all, which is said to obviate the need of expropriation of land and property. I suppose this means that employers would be taxed till they were too poor to employ; and then the State would employ. But what State—and, my God, what statesmen! Why, presumably (if *nothing* is needed but a new wage raised by a new tax) just the jolly statesmen the world produces at present, the parasitic Parliamentarians turned into omnipotent bureaucrats. I should refuse it, of course; first, because it preserves the wage-system; second because the worst wage-system is one with only one employer, who may be an omnipresent enemy; and third because, in the purely practical statement, there is no provision for any change in the type of tyrant. But this is unfair to the unpractical part; which of course is the better part. Mr. Murry does demand a terrific change of heart, though his scheme hardly ensures it. We may well struggle on as Distributists, when Communism seems so steep even to Communists; and they must endure the same abnormal austerity in order to be abnormal, that we endure to be normal.

In theory, or this part of his theory at least, Mr. Middleton Murry is an ascetic who wishes to transfer asceticism from the individual life, where it may be noble and beautiful, to the whole social and historical life, where it becomes simply vandalism or barbaric

---

[63] James Maxton (1885–1946) was a Scottish socialist who chaired the Independent Labour party in the late 1920s and again in the late 1930s. James Henry Thomas (1874–1949) was an English trade union leader who held cabinet positions under Ramsay MacDonald's Labour ministries.

destruction. In this he is undoubtedly at one with the Puritan or the Prohibitionist or the more mechanical sort of Pacifist; in short he is entirely at one with that sort of modern world which he most justly detests. Broadly considered, the fact that bulks biggest in the modern industrial world is this: that its moral movements are much *more* utterly and ruthlessly repressive than the past forms of mysticism or fanaticism that commonly affected only the few. Mediaeval men endured frightful fasts; but none of them would have dreamed of seriously proposing that nobody anywhere should ever have wine any more. And Prohibition, which was accepted by a huge modern industrial civilisation, did seriously propose that nobody should ever have wine any more. Cranks who dislike tobacco would utterly destroy all tobacco; I doubt whether they would even allow it medically as a sedative. Some Pagan sages and some Christian saints have been vegetarians, but nobody in the ancient world would ever have prophesied that flocks and herds would utterly vanish from the earth. But in the Utopia of the true vegetarian, I suppose they would utterly vanish from the earth. The more pedantic Pacifist has the same view of fighting, even for justice, and disarmament is as universal as conscription. For both conscription and disarmament are very modern notions. And modern notions of the sort are not only negative but nihilist; they always demand the absolute annihilation or "total prohibition" of something.

Now I am as adamant against Mr. Murry in this notion of mutilating our whole culture in a frenzy of moral renunciation. I admit that a saint may cut off his hand and enter heaven, and have a higher place there than the rest of us. But a plea for the amputation of the hands of all human beings, the vision of a Handless Humanity as the next evolutionary stage after that of the tailless ape, leaves me cold, however much it is commended as a splendid corporate self-sacrifice. These things are an allegory, in more ways than one. We may say indeed that the inhuman industrial era did really abolish the Hand, since it did abolish the Handicraft. I admit that monks have their own reasons for shaving their heads or nuns for cutting off their hair; but my advice to humanity outside such ecstasies would be to remain calm and keep its hair on. That a man should surrender his luxury is one thing; that mankind should surrender its liberty to deal with the problem of luxury is quite another. It is one thing to impoverish oneself; it is quite another responsibility to impoverish a whole cultural system of its culture. I might or might not be the better for giving up wine; I am absolutely certain that the world would not be better for giving up wine. Mr. Middleton Murry may be moved by a noble impulse to give up private property, but I do not for one single moment believe that humanity would be happier for giving up private property.

As a matter of fact, it is exactly this sort of sweeping destruction that has made it unhappy. The modern Capitalist world, which we unite to curse, actually came out of that notion of utterly abandoning the old for the promise of the new. Men said about the business of scarring English hills with rails or rolling English villages in smoke, exactly what Mr. Murry is now saying about sacrificing ancient faith or freedom and taxing moderate property out of existence. They said, as he does, that it was sad, that it was hard, that it called for a heroic sacrifice; but that we must not be sentimentalists clinging to the past, but must look to the brighter and broader future. And the brighter future was the epoch of Mr. Carnegie and Mr. Ford. Capitalism was actually founded by urging a new realism against an old romanticism. The answer is that it was not necessary for a whole society to give up beauty; and it is not necessary for a whole society to give up liberty. And if we look back at history, we shall see that these sweeping social renunciations have done nothing but harm. Over all America lies like an incubus the cold corpse of Puritanism, *because* one fervid generation thought that man must say farewell for ever to priests as well as play-actors, to sacraments as well as feasts. In short, men were asked to sacrifice everything for Calvinism as they are now asked to sacrifice everything for Communism. But though man may sacrifice anything, Everyman must not sacrifice everything. Individual men must sacrifice their own liberties, but only to restore liberty. And it is a grand irony that, while the cultured Communist (with all respect to him) is rending everybody else's garments and scattering ashes on other people's heads, away in many quiet places, on the hills of Lanark or deep in my own Buckingham beech-woods, priests and friars who have themselves renounced private property are rebuilding the farms and families of Distributism.

THE BACKWARD BOLSHIE

After all, the Bolshevist is really a Victorian. His is a nineteenth-century dream, even if it be a twentieth-century reality. It is notably so in the aspect which now makes the dream a nightmare; I mean the mad optimism about the advantages of machinery. What was offered to us as a Five Years Hence Plan ought really to have been called a Fifty Years Ago Plan. For they are only trying to do with Russia exactly what the Victorians did actually do with England; turn it into the workshop of the world and fill it with dirty tools and dismal mechanics. Marx was much more of a Victorian than Morris.[64] He may not have been technically a subject of Queen Victoria, though it is quite likely that he was. By geographical extraction I suppose he was a German—like Queen Victoria's husband and more remotely, Queen Victoria herself. By real or racial extraction he was a Jew; like Queen Victoria's favourite Prime Minister[65] and a good many other persons unnecessary to mention. But the late Victorian period was the very period at which the Jews, and especially the German Jews, were at the very top of their power and influence. From the time when they forced the Egyptian War[66] to the time when they forced the South African War,[67] they were imperial and immune. Certainly much more so than they are now; for the Jews are now being jumped on very unjustly in Germany itself, and old Victorians like Mr. Belloc and myself, who began in the days of Jewish omnipotence by attacking the Jews, will now probably die defending them. Anyhow, Karl Marx did not differ from any number of Victorian Jews in type or externals. He lived mostly in England, and launched his world religion from something more British than the British Empire: the British Museum. The Beard

---

[64] William Morris (1834–1896) was an English poet, novelist, artist and prominent advocate of socialism.

[65] Victoria's favorite prime minister was Benjamin Disraeli.

[66] Chesterton is referring to the British war against Egypt in 1882, a conflict prompted by the need to protect European investments.

[67] Chesterton is referring to the Boer War, 1899–1902.

which moves Mr. Wells to impatience was simply the beard of Victorian romance; the beard of Tennyson and Longfellow and Trollope. And though his plan has been very imperfectly applied in the one place in the world where he would have said it could not be applied at all (for this true Victorian saw the great commercial cities of Western Europe as the only possible battlefields of the future) it has all the character of a new and rather barbaric people imitating something that is already stale, not to say stinking, for civilised people. It was exactly like the very Victorian incident of the industrialising of Japan. That is, it was and is something essentially behind the times. The Japanese wear billycock hats presumably under the impression that we admire billycock hats. But, whatever just vengeance may fall upon our hats, this is to do an injustice to our heads. Now, as a matter of fact, our heads have in many ways advanced a little, since the days when our own Five Year Plan filled England with filth and smoke. Some rather deeper questions have arisen; questions about the individual, about the purpose of life, about religion in history, and so on. Philosophy, even Thomist philosophy, is heard again in Paris and Oxford.

Now Marx had no more philosophy than Macaulay. The Marxians therefore have no more philosophy than the Manchester School.[68] It was enough for Macaulay to rejoice in the mere excitement of extension, in the hope that "the roofs and chimneys of a new Manchester may rise in the wilds of Connemara." Similarly, it is enough for the Moscow Marxians to hope that the roofs and chimneys of a new Manchester may rise in the wilds of Siberia. It is true that the original Manchester men desired competition while the Marxians desire combination; or the Combine of all Combines. But the competition ended in a Combine and the Combine has not really ended in a Communist State. For it seems clear that grades of unequal wages do exist in Bolshevist Russia, and the Bolshevist rulers can only explain that it is a temporary necessity at this political stage and

---

[68] The Manchester School in mid-nineteenth-century England was a school of political economy associated with John Bright and Richard Cobden; it advocated free trade and government nonintervention in the economy.

that true, pure, perfect Communism will come in the future. It might be the Labour Party, mightn't it?

But to carry competition to any lengths, because it is the fashion, or to carry combination to any lengths because it is the fashion, is not a Philosophy. A philosophy begins with Being; with the end and value of a living thing; and it is manifest that a materialism that only considers economic ethics, cannot cover the question at all. If the problem of happiness were so solved by economic comfort, the classes who are now comfortable would be happy, which is absurd. This humourless hammering on one note is like the worst Victorian fads; Temperance or Feminism. It is especially like that very old-fashioned Feminism that hated to be feminine. I am told that in Russia men and women dress roughly alike. But, mark you, that does not mean that men wear flowers in their hair or trail about in those noble pontifical robes with which tradition clothed every woman like a queen. It means that women dress like men; not that men dress like women. Now that is sheer stark, stale, dead Victorianism. That is the only original Woman's Rights Woman, who deliberately made herself hideous with bloomers and goggles. By the following reigns, even the Suffragettes had learned better than that; but while the Suffragettes are things of the past for us, they are still far in the rosy future for the backward and belated Bolshevist. He is still plodding through that foggy factory twilight that was supposed to be the enlightened daylight of the nineteenth century; and it is truer now than in the time of the Czars to say that Russia is the most backward of the nations.

THE LAST TURN

The only difficulty about the evident reawakening of Catholicism in modern England, is that conversion calls on a man to stretch his mind, as a man awakening from a sleep may stretch his arms and legs. It calls on the imagination to stretch itself, for instance, over a wider area than England, and a longer period than English history. And, for certain rather curious reasons, the stretching of the mind generally stops short of anything like a complete comprehension of any great historical or philosophical process. This is what Bernard Shaw meant when he said that the world will never really progress, until every man lives for three hundred years. I remember remarking at the time that there was a sort of truth symbolised in this; and that, most certainly, if Bernard Shaw had lived for three hundred years he would be a Catholic.

This preliminary point can be quite sufficiently proved even from this particular case. Three hundred years would mean that he would remember, as part of the positive poetry of childhood, the first phase of the Reformation. The first phase of the Reformation in England was the Divine Right of Kings. It was a romantic enthusiasm for Royalty itself, and the duty of an utterly prostrate passive obedience to it. This was the first effect of the New Religion; but before the child was barely a boy it would be overthrown by another New Religion. The Calvinist killed the sacred King, who had been sacred enough to kill the Church; and darkened the land with a creed of Total Depravity and the Scottish Sabbath. By the time Mr. Shaw was a growing lad of only a hundred years old, the world would have rebelled against this tyranny in turn. The Scottish Mr. Hume would soon be preparing to burst up the Scottish Sabbath. The ingenious Mr. Rousseau would be denying Total Depravity and asserting Total Innocence, Naturalness and Niceness. Out of this, as he grew to maturity, nearing a century and a half, there would grow gradually the most pleasant and plausible, the most happy, healthy and exhilarating of all the purely human visions: the vision of Liberty. Let men be only free from their feudal chains and theological gags;

let them speak as they like, write as they like, buy and sell as they like, trade and travel and enquire as they like; and the race will waken from the nightmare of ages into the broad brotherhood of reason and justice. About the time when Mr. Shaw's first grey hair appeared, in the year 1832, when he was barely two hundred, there was much talk about a Reform Bill in England; but I do not think Mr. Shaw would have been taken in, even then. Already, for a long time, men had been buying and selling as they liked, and trading and travelling as they liked. And already the result stood up solid and enormous, in the thing called Capitalism: that is the dispossession of the populace of all forms of real productive property; all instruments of production in the hands of the few; all the millions merely the servants of the few, working for a wage, always an insecure wage, generally a mean and inhuman wage. It was when this process had gone even further that the real historical Mr. Bernard Shaw was born; with the natural consequence that Mr. Bernard Shaw has devoted his life to making war on Capitalism. He has done so because the special evil of his own lifetime was Capitalism. But shall we not guess that he would have done it rather differently, if he had already spent two or three lifetimes warring against Divine Right, and then against the Calvinism that attacked Divine Right, and then against the Rousseauan prostration before Liberty, which destroyed Calvinism—and produced Capitalism. Would he not conclude that the whole State had been staggering about in a most extraordinary and irrational manner, ever since he was first born under the Elizabethan Settlement? Would it not be obvious that the mind of man had been filled with nothing but frantic exaggerations, crude simplifications, provincial panaceas and quack medicines and sheer raving monomania, ever since it had broken away from the central civilisation and the philosophy which the Saints had handed down from the Ancients? Would it not interest him to find that, all the time, there had been written in the open books of Aquinas or Bellarmine or Suarez,[69] a perfectly reasonable apportionment of the authority of princes, the claims of peoples,

---

[69] Francisco Suarez (1548–1617) was a Spanish Jesuit and neoscholastic theologian.

the possibilities of democracy, the use and abuse of property, and
the right function of freedom?

Three hundred years felt with their full weight, really measured
out in time and experience, endured as a man actually endures the
passage of his days, would prove the whole Protestant story to have
been the most preposterous and disproportionate detour, or strag-
gling a chapter of accidents, that ever set out in the wrong direction
and came back to the same place. For we have in a hundred ways
come back to the same place; even to the detail of an exaggerated
reaction, like that of the *Action Française*,[70] renewing the absolute
appeal to The King. And nothing is more amusing than to note the
way in which those who regard themselves as the most advanced
leaders, of the most modern groups, are already rearing and bucking
against the whole tendency of liberal and humanitarian progress, which
the last revolutionary leaders marked out for them. Nobody is less
in the spirit of Walt Whitman than Wyndham Lewis[71] or T. S. Eliot;
nobody less a real heir of H. G. Wells than Aldous Huxley; nobody
less disposed to follow the humanitarian paths of Mr. Nevinson the
adventurous journalist, than his son Mr. Nevinson[72] the Futurist
painter. All these of the most recent school of rebels are rebelling
against rebellion; that is, against the Revolution and all its heritage
of liberty, equality and fraternity. Mr. Eliot, though an American, is
an avowed Royalist. Mr. Nevinson has become a quite ferocious
Kiplingite Imperialist. Mr. Wyndham Lewis seems to prefer a Dictatorship, in so far as he may be said to prefer anything. All this last
turn of the twisting road of progress is pointing back towards what
we have called for a hundred years reaction. It is apparent in the

[70] Action Française was a French monarchist group that flourished in the 1920s
and 1930s under the leadership of the poet and journalist Charles Maurras (1868–1952).

[71] Percy Wyndham Lewis (1884–1957) was an English novelist, critic and painter
involved in avant-garde artistic movements.

[72] Henry Wood Nevinson (1856–1941) was an English journalist and war correspondent during the Boer War and campaigns in the Balkans and Dardanelles. In
1904 he exposed the Portuguese slave trade in Angola. His son, Christopher
Nevinson (1889–1946), achieved fame as a Futurist painter and an official war artist;
his war pictures were exhibited in London in 1916.

Fascists; in the Hitlerites; and even in the open anti-democracy of the Bolshevists.

Now the great danger of the moment is that young men will go on being content with these revolts against revolt, these reactions against reactions; so that we have nothing but an everlasting seesaw of the Old Young and the New Young; the last always content with its fleeting triumph over the last but one. And the only way to avoid that result is to teach men to stretch their minds and inhabit a larger period of time. It is to insist, not that we now feel inclined to stress this or stress that, in mere fashion or mere fatigue, but that there really does exist somewhere a reasonable plan of the proportions of things, which, at least in its general outline, is true all the time. The moment men, so intelligent as those I have named, begin to realise that this permanent plan is necessary, they will certainly realise that the only existing plan, that has any plausible claim to look like it, is the plan of the Catholic Faith. For the present, they seem to be quite content to continue the old squabble of fathers and sons; even if the fathers are very young fathers, or the sons actually appeal to the grandfathers against them. But this merely modern squabble is after all local and therefore provincial; it can never satisfy the thirst of thinking people for the reality of things. Nevertheless, as I stated at the beginning, the great difficulty is whether a man can stretch his mind, or (as the moderns would say) can broaden his mind, enough to see the need for an eternal Church.

And yet surely this is only the last lap in the long race in which the ancient truth, so heavily handicapped, has one by one outdistanced all the runners who prided themselves on their youth or their advance positions. If a man could have learned it by a process of elimination, merely by living through the last three hundred years, he would learn the same lesson even more clearly by living through the next three hundred years. By that time it will be more apparent than ever that these jerks of novelty do not create either a progress or an equilibrium. The very newest of the intellectuals have already learnt not to trust to mere progress, in the sense of a process of change; they already know that they have sometimes more in common with some antique authority than with some merely modern

rebellion. Some of them would set up Dictators to enforce obedience; it is hard if we may not obey willingly, when they would have
men obey even unwillingly. They would set up violent authority in
the hands of individuals; they can hardly complain if we recognise
merely moral authority in a merely mystical office. For that mystical
office contains all the liberties and all the philosophies, and judges
only upon their right balance and proportion; and every other thing
that the moderns call a movement is only securing for a monomania
the brief life of a sect.

THE NEW LUTHER

It seems that there is some movement or other, of a religious sort; which, being founded by a Lutheran of German race and American origin, naturally connects itself with the name of Oxford. Some people say it is called the Oxford Group Movement. Other people seem to be somewhat needlessly alarmed, lest it be identified by historians with the Oxford Movement. I would suggest, in a friendly spirit, that it should be called the Oxford Street Movement. Oxford Street does actually contain the name of the University town, which seems to be all that is required; and at the same time, it is a long way from Oxford. I think the atmosphere there would be more congruous and comfortable; and somehow I feel that Mr. Gordon Selfridge,[73] being in the neighbourhood, would be more really sympathetic and spiritually helpful than the Master of Balliol.

When I had made some such idle jest I received a letter of remonstrance against what I had written of the Buchman Group Movement.[74] The letter was written in a pained and almost pathetic tone, expressing regret that I should depreciate anything that brought men back to the reality of religion; and I ought at least to assure the writer that I am not insensible to any such plea. In this as in many things, however, religion is treated in a curious manner, as distinct from politics or ethics or economics. Nobody says that because all political parties may be presumed to contain many well-wishers to the public good, therefore we must not resist Communism or attack Capitalism, or express our trust or distrust of Fascism. The roads which lead to different social solutions are recognised as divergent. It is only the paths to hell and heaven of which it is enough to say

[73] Gordon Selfridge (1858–1947) was an American businessman who moved to England in 1906 and opened a popular department store in London.

[74] The Buchman Group Movement, better known as Moral Re-armament (the name it took in 1938), was founded in the 1920s by the American Frank Buchman (1878–1961). It was a nondenominational religious movement that sought to change the world order by persuading individuals to confess their sins and follow God's guidance. These confessions took place at "house parties".

that they are paved with good intentions. Let me say at once that I do sympathise with any sinners who seek such an outlet; even with the rather exclusive and arrogant spiritual aristocracy which writes over its gates, "For Sinners Only." I sympathise with them, not so much as I sympathise with the ignorant fishermen bawling hymns in any dingy old chapel in any Devonshire fishing village; not quite so much as I sympathise with a company of Holy Rollers rolling on the ground in the neighbourhood of Dayton, Tennessee,[75] to avert the curse of Evolution; and not half so much as I sympathise with Moslem fakirs howling in the desert and shaking their splendid spears and dying on the British bayonets. But I do sympathise with all these people; since they are all seeking God. And I am sufficiently orthodox to know that, in some mystical way beyond our measurement, it is true that seeking is finding.

But if my correspondent, or anybody else, wishes to know why I rather prefer the followers of the Mad Mullah to the followers of Herr Buchman, he will find it perfectly summed up in an interview and article which appeared in the *News-Chronicle* and was headed in huge letters with the words, "Vision of a New Reformation: Group Leader's Hope from Germany." He will find it exquisitely and exactly concentrated, as in the crystallization of a gem, in these words; read them; re-read them; ponder them. They contain the whole substance of the subject. "These Groupers think on a large scale. The Canadians, for instance, have not only booked the Chateau Frontenac for a houseparty of 3,000 at Quebec next year, but have already chartered a C.P.R. liner to bring their contingent to England for the next Oxford houseparty."

That, you will observe, is thinking largely. To rude, rustic, Distributist minds, it would not appear that it is thinking at all. There have been any number of sectarians and Puritan fanatics who have very genuinely thought; some who have thought and thought until they went mad. But I should say that the sanity and solidity of the Group Movement was quite safe from any such danger as that. Note

---

[75] Dayton, Tennessee, was the site of the Scopes trial of evolutionary theory, in 1925.

that it is not a question of whether religion may think too much about pomp and grandeur. It is a question of whether religion is to boast of having pomp without thinking at all. There is a real case to be made out both for and against the most Pagan phase of the Papacy, which filled Rome with trophies that might have stood for the triumphs of Trajan or Augustus. But it does need some thought to build even a Pagan temple or erect even an Imperialistic monument. The dome which Michelangelo made the culmination of St. Peter's is not only a large dome. It is a dome made by a man who was thinking largely. Nay, it might have been less large if it had been larger. Lift it a little higher in the air and the curve is constricted; spread it a little wider and the curve is flattened. That is what is meant by thinking; and especially by thinking largely. At any rate, it is a rather different operation from buying up somebody else's steamboat, or securing all the beds in somebody else's hotel.

Finally, what shall we say in the light (or twilight) of all this, of the magnificent claim made in such large letters that they would cover a whole paragraph of this essay; the "Vision of a New Reformation: Group Leader's Hope from Germany"? We may say this to begin with; that here, as in every single thing I have read about the Group Movement, as in every page and paragraph of the book called *For Sinners Only*, there is an extraordinary ambiguity. What is meant by a New Reformation? What is it that is to be reformed? Is it just possible that it is the Reformation that is to be reformed? And, for those who have a pedantic fancy for looking at the structure of the words they write or speak, into what form is it to be reformed? Can it be into the old original form? Certainly in all this there is no trace or outline of any new form. Or does it mean by a New Reformation, a repetition of the Reformation? Does it mean an extension of the Reformation? Does it mean that we are to look for somebody who shall be more Lutheran than Luther? I suppose the real doctrine of the great Reformer might possibly be pushed further than he pushed it. It is very difficult to imagine any doctrine that could make man more base, describe human nature as more desperately impotent, blacken the reason and the will of man with a more utterly bottomless and hopeless despair than did the real doctrine of Luther. But it may be that there are depths below the depths and that it is possible to damn the dignity of Adam more completely than Luther damned it. Is that what is meant by a New Reformation? That is the only Reformation that would bear the remotest resemblance to the old Reformation. But that is just the difficulty; and that is just the point. I cannot accuse the Buchmanites of repeating the Lutheran pessimism. I cannot accuse them of revolting against the Lutheran pessimism. The very language they use is so loose and vague and journalistic, that it might mean either that the New Reformation is to restore Luther or reverse Luther. All they are sure about is that it will come from Germany, like Luther—or like Hitler. There is a certain intellectual courage, which some would call impudence, about saying at this moment that the Vision of a New Reformation is of necessity a Hope from Germany. It is amusing to read it at the very moment when even the Pro-Germans have begun to think that Germany is hopeless. Anyhow, the religious leader in question is welcome, so far as I am concerned, to any New Reformation which puts the Swastika above the Cross and teaches men first to be very arrogant Germans before it allows them to be very apologetic Christians. All that may be a reformation in the sense of a new form; but it seems to me, on the side of religious thought, to be the very essence of formlessness.

BABIES AND DISTRIBUTISM

I hope it is not a secret arrogance to say that I do not think I am exceptionally arrogant; or if I were, my religion would prevent me from being proud of my pride. Nevertheless, for those of such a philosophy, there is a very terrible temptation to intellectual pride, in the welter of wordy and worthless philosophies that surround us today. Yet there are not many things that move me to anything like a personal contempt. I do not feel any contempt for an atheist, who is often a man limited and constrained by his own logic to a very sad simplification. I do not feel any contempt for a Bolshevist, who is a man driven to the same negative simplification by a revolt against very positive wrongs. But there is one type of person for whom I feel what I can only call contempt. And that is the popular propagandist of what he or she absurdly describes as Birth-Control.

I despise Birth-Control first because it is a weak and wobbly and cowardly word. It is also an entirely meaningless word; and is used so as to curry favour even with those who would at first recoil from its real meaning. The proceeding these quack doctors recommend does not *control* any birth. It only makes sure that there shall never be any birth to control. It cannot, for instance, determine sex, or even make any selection in the style of the pseudo-science of Eugenics. Normal people can only act so as to produce birth; and these people can only act so as to prevent birth. But these people know perfectly well that they dare not write the plain word Birth-Prevention, in any one of the hundred places where they write the hypocritical word Birth-Control. They know as well as I do that the very word Birth-Prevention would strike a chill into the public, the instant it was blazoned on headlines, or proclaimed on platforms, or scattered in advertisements like any other quack medicine. They dare not call it by its name, because its name is very bad advertising. Therefore they use a conventional and unmeaning word, which may make the quack medicine sound more innocuous.

Second, I despise Birth-Control because it is a weak and wobbly and cowardly thing. It is not even a step along the muddy road they call Eugenics; it is a flat refusal to take the first and most obvious step along the road of Eugenics. Once grant that their philosophy is right, and their course of action is obvious; and they dare not take it; they dare not even declare it. If there is no authority in things which Christendom has called moral, because their origins were mystical, then they are clearly free to ignore all difference between animals and men; and treat men as we treat animals. They need not palter with the stale and timid compromise and convention called Birth-Control. Nobody applies it to the cat. The obvious course for Eugenists is to act towards babies as they act towards kittens. Let all the babies be born; and then let us drown those we do not like. I cannot see any objection to it; except the moral or mystical sort of objection that we advance against Birth-Prevention. And that would be real and even reasonable Eugenics; for we could then select the best, or at least the healthiest, and sacrifice what are called the unfit. By the weak compromise of Birth-Prevention, we are very probably sacrificing the fit and only producing the unfit. The births we prevent may be the births of the best and most beautiful children; those we allow, the weakest or worst. Indeed, it is probable; for the habit discourages the early parentage of young and vigorous people; and lets them put off the experience to later years, mostly from mercenary motives. Until I see a real pioneer and progressive leader coming out with a good, bold, scientific programme for drowning babies, I will not join the movement.

But there is a third reason for my contempt, much deeper and therefore much more difficult to express; in which is rooted all my reasons for being anything I am or attempt to be; and above all, for being a Distributist. Perhaps the nearest to a description of it is to say this: that my contempt boils over into bad behaviour when I hear the common suggestion that a birth is avoided because people want to be "free" to go to the cinema or buy a gramophone or a loud-speaker. What makes me want to walk over such people like doormats is that they use the word "free." By every act of that sort they chain themselves to the most servile and mechanical system yet tolerated by men. The cinema is a machine for unrolling certain regular patterns called pictures; expressing the most vulgar millionaires' notion of the taste of the most vulgar millions. The gramophone is a machine for recording such tunes as certain shops and other organisations choose to sell. The wireless is better; but even that is marked by the modern mark of all three; the impotence of the receptive party. The amateur cannot challenge the actor; the householder will find it vain to go and shout into the gramophone; the mob cannot pelt the modern speaker, especially when he is a loud-speaker. It is all a central mechanism giving out to men exactly what their masters think they should have.

Now a child is the very sign and sacrament of personal freedom. He is a fresh free will added to the wills of the world; he is something that his parents have freely chosen to produce and which they freely agree to protect. They can feel that any amusement he gives (which is often considerable) really comes from him and from them, and from nobody else. He has been born without the intervention of any master or lord. He is a creation and a contribution; he is their own creative contribution to creation. He is also a much more beautiful, wonderful, amusing and astonishing thing than any of the stale stories or jingling jazz tunes turned out by the machines. When men no longer feel that he is so, they have lost the appreciation of primary things, and therefore all sense of proportion about the world. People who prefer the mechanical pleasures, to such a miracle, are jaded and enslaved. They are preferring the very dregs of life to the first fountains of life. They are preferring the last, crooked, indirect, borrowed, repeated and exhausted things of our dying Capitalist civilisation, to the reality which is the only rejuvenation of all civilisation. It is they who are hugging the chains of their old slavery; it is the child who is ready for the new world.

THREE FOES OF THE FAMILY

It was certainly a very brilliant lightning-flash of irony by which Mr. Aldous Huxley lit up the whole loathsome landscape of his satirical Utopia, of synthetic humanity and manufactured men and women, by the old romantic quotation of "Brave New World". The quotation comes, of course, from that supreme moment of the magic of youth, nourished by the magic of old age, when Miranda[76] the marvellous becomes Miranda the marvelling, at the unique wonder of first love. To use it for the very motto of a system which, having lost all innocence, would necessarily lose all wonder, was a touch of very withering wit. And yet it will be well to remember that, in comparison with some other worlds, where the same work is done more weakly and quite as wickedly, the Utopia of the extremists really has something of the intellectual integrity which belongs to extremes, even of madness. In that sense the two ironical adjectives are not merely ironical. The horrible human, or inhuman, hive described in Mr. Huxley's romance is certainly a base world, and a filthy world, and a fundamentally unhappy world. But it is in one sense a new world; and it is in one sense a brave world. At least a certain amount of bravery, as well as brutality, would have to be shown before anything of the sort could be established in the world of fact. It would need some courage, and even some self-sacrifice, to establish anything so utterly disgusting as that.

But the same work is being done in other worlds that are not particularly new, and not in the least brave. These are people of another sort, much more common and conventional, who are not only working to create such a paradise of cowardice, but who actually try to work for it through a conspiracy of cowards. The attitude of these people towards the Family and the tradition of its Christian virtues is the attitude of men willing to wound and yet afraid to strike; or ready to sap and mine so long as they are not called upon to fire or fight in the open. And those who do this cover much

---

[76] Miranda is a character in Shakespeare's *The Tempest*.

more than half, or nearly two-thirds, of the people who write in the most respectable and conventional Capitalist newspapers. It cannot be too often repeated that what destroyed the Family in the modern world was Capitalism. No doubt it might have been Communism, if Communism had ever had a chance, outside that semi-Mongolian wilderness where it actually flourishes. But, so far as we are concerned, what has broken up households, and encourages divorces, and treated the old domestic virtues with more and more open contempt, is the epoch and power of Capitalism. It is Capitalism that has forced a moral feud and a commercial competition between the sexes; that has destroyed the influence of the parent in favour of the influence of the employer; that has driven men from their homes to look for jobs; that has forced them to live near their factories or their firms instead of near their families; and, above all, that has encouraged, for commercial reasons, a parade of publicity and garish novelty, which is in its nature the death of all that was called dignity and modesty by our mothers and fathers. It is not the Bolshevist but the Boss, the publicity man, the salesman and the commercial advertiser who have, like a rush and riot of barbarians, thrown down and trampled under foot the ancient Roman statue of Verecundia.[77] But because the thing is done by men of this sort, of course it is done in their own muggy and muddle-headed way; by all the irresponsible tricks of their foul Suggestion and their filthy Psychology. It is done, for instance, by perpetually guying the old Victorian virtues or limitations which, as they are no longer there, are not likely to retaliate. It is done more by pictures than by printed words; because printed words are supposed to make some sense and a man may be answerable for printing them. Stiff and hideous effigies of women in crinolines or bonnets are paraded, as if *that* could possibly be all there was to see when Maud[78] came into the garden, and was saluted by such a song. Fortunately, Maud's friends, who would have challenged the pressman and photographer to a duel, are all dead; and these satirists of Victorianism are very careful to find out that all their enemies are

[77] The statue depicts Modesty.
[78] *Maud* is a poetic monodrama published by Tennyson in 1855.

dead. Some of their bold caricaturists have been known to charge an old-fashioned bathing-machine as courageously as if it were a machine-gun. It is convenient thus courageously to attack bathing-machines, because there are no bathing-machines to attack. Then they balance these things by photographs of the Modern Girl at various stages of the nudist movement; and trust that anything so obviously vulgar is bound to be popular. For the rest, the Modern Girl is floated on a sea of sentimental sloppiness; a continuous gush about her frankness and freshness, the perfect naturalness of her painting her face or the unprecedented courage of her having no children. The whole is diluted with a dreary hypocrisy about comradeship, far more sentimental than the old-fashioned sentiment. When I see the Family sinking in these swamps of amorphous amorous futility, I feel inclined to say, "Give me the Communists." Better Bolshevist battles and the Brave New World than the ancient house of man rotted away silently by such worms of secret sensuality and individual appetite. "The coward does it with a kiss; the brave man with a sword." [79]

But there is, curiously enough, a third thing of the kind, which I am really inclined to think that I dislike even more than the other two. It is not the Communist attacking the family or the Capitalist betraying the family; it is the vast and very astonishing vision of the Hitlerite defending the family. Hitler's way of defending the independence of the family is to make every family dependent on him and his semi-Socialist State; and to preserve the authority of parents by authoritatively telling all the parents what to do. His notion of keeping sacred the dignity of domestic life is to issue peremptory orders that the grandfather is to get up at five in the morning and do dumb-bell exercises, or the grandmother to march twenty miles to a camp to procure a Swastika flag. In other words, he appears to interfere with family life more even than the Bolshevists do; and to do it in the name of the sacredness of the family. It is not much more encouraging than the other two social manifestations; but at least it is more entertaining.

[79] The quotation is from Oscar Wilde's *The Ballad of Reading Gaol* (1898).

THE DON AND THE CAVALIER

Mr. Christopher Hollis has written an excellent book on John Dryden. It is an instructive book; it is also an amusing book; but not so amusing as some of the reviews of it. And it concerns me here, at the moment mainly in relation to the general position to-day of the school of academic critics, who have upheld for so long a time the historical theory which is often called Parliamentarism and is in fact Plutocracy. It is of some moment to the Distributist movement because it was the official defence of this policy which made possible the dispossession of the populace. Now about the present position of that official criticism there are several rather curious things to note. The first is its *tone*; which is quite queer in its difference from the tone used in my youth, when historians were as simple as Macaulay; I might almost say when scholars were as ignorant as Macaulay. For a man can be very learned and very ignorant; and Macaulay achieved the combination to the admiration of heaven and earth. Macaulay would make short work, or imagine that he could make short work, of any young man who played at being a Jacobite;[80] he was impatient with him as with a crank; but he was *honestly* impatient; his impatience was a sort of innocence. The critics on the same side to-day have lost their innocence. They know perfectly well that they have been defeated in battle after battle upon the big facts; and they have a curious carefulness in dealing only with very small facts. Anybody who said thirty years ago that Charles the First was not in fact a tyrant, dethroned by an indignant democracy, could really be treated as a sort of Mr. Dick,[81] with a weakness for weeping over King Charles's Head. The modern critic does not really dare to-day to appear as the executioner (even though the critic, like the executioner, can wear a mask and remain nameless); he has not now the

[80] A Jacobite was a partisan of the Stuart cause after the deposing of James II in 1688.

[81] Mr. Dick is a character in Charles Dicken's David Copperfield, written in 1849–1850.

nerve to shake King Charles's Head at the people and shout confi-
dently, "Behold the Head of a Traitor." So he becomes more fussy
and particular than ever over the ancient, profound, pressing and
all-important question: "Out of which window in Whitehall did
Charles the First step to have his head cut off?" And that, as Disraeli
very truly observed, is one of the two or three quite infallible ways
of becoming a bore.

And the new professor of the old history is rather a bore; but
what is much worse, he is a nervous bore. He not only drawls, but
he also stammers. And his tone, as I have said, has achieved a most
peculiar accent of acrid timidity. I read one criticism of Mr. Hollis's
book, in a highly learned and authoritative weekly; and it largely
left me wondering whether the critic who wrote it had read that
particular passage in it, in which Mr. Hollis, contrasting the methods of Dryden and Pope, quotes the whole of the latter poet's famous
satire upon Addison. Whether or no it was like Addison, it was
exactly like the critic.[82]

> "Willing to wound and yet afraid to strike,
> Just hint a doubt and hesitate dislike;
> Damn with faint praise, assent with civil leer,
> And without sneering teach the rest to sneer."

Again, over and above this unmistakable tone, there is the change in
the method which I have compared to the change from laughing at
Mr. Dick over King Charles's Head to quarrelling about which win-
dowsill had the honour to be bestridden by King Charles's legs. There
was an excellent example in this review, of the method of avoiding
battle on the main issue and picking a quarrel about a trifle. Mr.
Hollis made the general remark, which is a true and valuable remark,
that it is rather a disadvantage of revolutions that they often have to
be followed by new and rigid repressions, set up by the revolution-
ists themselves. He gives the example that William of Orange's government censored a sort of controversy which under the last Stuarts
was much more free. The critic then suggested that the whole book

[82] The quotation is from Pope's "Epistle to Dr. Arbuthnot" (1735).

and its author were historically unreliable, upon some verbal inter-
pretation of William of Orange's government; because the censorship
was removed later; I think in 1695. The point of general interest is that
there was a new censorship; and the critic's way of proving that there
was not a censorship is to say that there was a censorship, that lasted
for about eight years. Now Mr. Hollis's general philosophy may be right
or wrong; but Mr. Hollis's general remark was perfectly philosophical
and a quite reasonable comment on this and many other cases of the
same truth. The critic's correction, if his correction is correct, is not
of the slightest philosophical or rational interest to anybody; it has no
relation to the point that was really raised; it only says that somebody
did something, but did not do it all the time. That is what I mean by
the one side being concerned with triviality and the other side with
truth. Mr. Hollis's suggestion is of some intelligent importance to us,
who are living among real revolutions; Bolshevist revolutions or
Hitlerite revolutions. It is not necessarily a complete condemnation
of revolutions. It is simply a note on the natural history of revolu-
tionists. But his history really is natural history, and the academic and
pedantic history has become utterly unnatural.

There is a saying that a great silence broods over the great battlefields. There is certainly a very astounding silence over the great
recent defeats of the Orangemen's theory of history. Mr. Hollis begins
his book by noting the picturesque coincidence that Dryden sat fishing in the river upon which Mary Stuart had looked out from the
Tower of Fotheringay.[83] The storming and taking of that Tower,
with all its secrets, was a struggle that once made an amazing noise,
that has now been followed by a more amazing stillness. Hardly anything is said about its sensational termination; simply because the
main part of the old accepted case against the Catholic Queen has
completely broken down. Considering how frightfully important it
was that the Casket Letters[84] were all certainly genuine, it is very
funny to find how unimportant it is that they are most of them

[83] Mary Stuart was imprisoned in Fotheringay castle in 1586, tried for her role in
a plot to assassinate Elizabeth, and executed in 1587.

[84] The Casket Letters, purportedly written by Mary Stuart, implicated her in the
murder of her husband, Lord Darnley.

probably forgeries. The war was so fierce and ruthless while they thought they were winning it; it is so very quiet and casual and gentlemanly, now that they know they are losing it. That intellectual interlude at least is over; England is returning to her own past, and could hardly march under a better battle-sign than what Macaulay himself had the magnanimity to call "the towering crest of Dryden."

I also came upon another critique of the book on Dryden; and one which goes far beyond the sort of negative hostility in the critics which I have criticised. That was, after all, only the confession that the Whig and Puritan school of history is fighting the rearguard action of a retreat, and that it mostly consists of rather futile sniping. Instead of the old uproarious cannonade of Macaulay, we do now in practice only "hear the distant and random gun that the foe is sullenly firing." But the later criticism involved something more universal and significant than that. It really did represent the amazing, mystifying and in some ways almost exciting muddle, in what calls itself the Modern Mind. I say exciting, because when a mystification becomes as mad as that, it has almost the character of a mystery story; it is as if the modern man must have had a knock on the head, and we were all detectives trying to find out who really did it. How did it really happen that the cultivated, sometimes even the classical critic of this particular period, suffers from a heavy blow from some blunt instrument, so that he thinks and writes in the following fashion?

The critic in question said in these words, or almost these words: "We have no reason to doubt the sincerity of Dryden's conversion to Roman Catholicism; but, after all, in the case of so great a man as Dryden, does the question matter very much?" That is the Modern Mind. This is the forest primeval, the murmuring pines and the hemlocks. This is the Jungle. This is the thickest of all thickets and the thorniest of all earthly briar-patches; and though I was born and bred in that briar-patch, like Brer Rabbit, I found it difficult to discover a path out of it; and I did not know how we are really to make a path through it.

Of course we can always begin by using the primitive implement of reason; and try to let in a little light merely by letting in a little logic. So far as I understand the argument as an argument, it is this. If John Dryden had been born half-witted, or if he had been a dunce and a dull fellow entirely insignificant in the intellectual and social life of his time—*then* it would have been frightfully and sensationally important to know whether he was or was not sincere, with a soul-searching sincerity, in his intellectual acceptance of the complete Catholic philosophy. But as he was not a dunce but a poet, as he was not a half-wit but a wit, as he was not a mindless person but a very great mind, then it must be a matter of indifference whether such an intellect can accept such an intellectual philosophy. Dryden was so great a thinker that it does not matter what he thought; he was almost certainly in search of the truth, but he was so capable of searching for it that nobody can take any interest in whether he found it; and it is only in the case of a small man that we could take a great interest in the great truth that he thought he found. How, I ask you, do people get their minds into a tangle like that? How could a man be sincere in his Catholicism, and yet think himself superior to his Catholicism? How could his greatness be detached from anything so great as a belief in a universal order of life, death and eternity; if he really had the greatness and really had the belief? It might make some sense if Dryden was not sincere; but it is practically admitted that he was sincere. It might make some sense if Dryden was small; but it is actually based on the view that he was great.

While the world has been talking about removing Victorian taboos, I have been resolved from the first to remove that one Victorian taboo; which really was a senseless and strangling taboo; the taboo on the *topic* of real religion, and its real and inevitable place in practical life. Most of the things the Moderns call Victorian taboos are about as Victorian as the Ten Commandments or the maxims of Confucius. But this really was Victorian, in the sense of having arisen recently in a vulgar, commercial and cowardly social system. It is not the notion that it is right or wrong to be a Moslem; it is the notion that it cannot really matter even to a Moslem that he is a Moslem. What is totally intolerable is the idea that everybody must pretend, for the sake of peace and decorum, that moral inspiration only comes from secular things like Distributism, and cannot possibly come from spiritual things like Catholicism. That is the fixed idea like a fossil that lies under all the labyrinthine wrappings or coil of contradictory conventions, in the mind of the reviewer whose words I quote.

It has nothing to do with what he would call being religious; or forcing religion upon him or anybody else. No Catholic thinks he is a good Catholic; or he would by that thought become a bad Catholic. I for one am not even tempted to any illusion in that matter; I fear that very often, when I have got up early to go to Mass, I have said with a groan, *Tantum religio potuit suadere malorum*, which, I may explain to the Moslem, is not a quotation from the Mass. But the critic here in question does not say, in the grand Lucretian manner, "Religion alone can persuade men to such evils." He says, "Religion alone cannot really have persuaded anybody to anything." He stands for a stupid interlude of intellectual history, in which men would not recognise religion either as a friend or an enemy, which supposed that a great man must be great, not merely in spite of it, but even without reference to it. That intellectual interlude was never very intellectual; and anyhow, it is over.

THE CHURCH AND AGORAPHOBIA

The erection of a great cathedral in a great city, and especially in a great port, that is a city that is also a wide gate of the world, recalls certain truths that are curiously forgotten, or sometimes still more astonishingly contradicted or reversed. Before we come to count the million mistakes and misunderstandings which separate men from the Catholic Church, there is one enormous and elementary mistake, which has to do with this question of scale and position in the world. To put it shortly; the man who fears to enter the Church commonly fancies that what he feels is a sort of claustrophobia. As a fact, what he really feels, is rather a sort of agoraphobia. Some silly little historical accidents, almost entirely peculiar to the particular way in which Catholicism survived in England, have given many Englishmen an extraordinary notion that it is a sort of hole and corner affair. These honest Protestants, like the imaginary nuns in the impossible romances, walk about in perpetual fear of being "walled up." For them the typical Catholic act is not going into a great thing like a church, but into a small thing like a confessional box. And to their nightmare fancy a confessional box is a sort of mantrap; and presents in its very appearance some combination of a coffin and a cage. The same notion is reinforced by the use of the word "cells," which in a Protestant community means prison-cells, and not monastic cells. The same is suggested by the word "crypt," about which there must obviously be something cryptic. These and many other tags of tradition have preserved in this country the custom of talking as if the danger of being a Catholic was the danger of being buried in a deep dark hole. And yet even the tradition was, not only a legend, but very nearly a pretence. Even the man who said these things knew in his heart, or at least had a vague knowledge at the back of his mind, that his fear was really a fear of something larger than himself and his tribal traditions; that he was really, as it was sometimes stated from both points of view, leaving a national for an international church. As I have said, it was not claustrophobia, the fear of the crypt or the cell; it was agoraphobia, or the fear of the

forum, of the market-place, of the open spaces and the colossal public buildings. To the really insular and individualistic type of sectarian, even the fear of the Church was also partly a fear of the world.
It can be seen in the terror which some of the English Tories, in the
old times, felt towards the cosmopolitan culture of the Jesuits; who
honestly seemed to them a sort of universal anarchists. It can be
seen in the exaggerated revulsion from the very varied experiments,
failures and successes of the Baroque. Of nearly all the non-Catholic
types of our time we can truly say, that any such type must broaden
his mind to become a Catholic. He must grow more used than he is
at present to the long avenues and the large spaces. This is really
what is meant by the Puritans who say that the Church is Pagan;
that it does open a very long avenue, which is the only avenue left
connecting us with Pagan antiquity. That is largely what is meant by
insisting that the Church covers all sorts of dubious or disreputable
people; all the motley mobs of tramps and pedlars and beggars, who
do make up the life of an open market-place. *Quicquid agunt homines;*[85] which even Matthew Arnold wisely saw was the true motto
of the practical life of the Roman Catholic Church.

Now a great deal has been said by Protestants, naturally enough,
and not a little even by Catholics, about the danger of displaying
before the world a pomp and triumph that may easily be called worldly.
Undoubtedly some harm was done, and some misunderstandings did
arise, when the Popes of the Renaissance filled Rome with trophies
that might have marked the triumphs of the Caesars, and permitted
the slander that the father of Christian man had usurped the title of
King of Kings and forgotten his own actual title of Servant of Servants. But, taking human nature as a whole, the method is justified;
because it is some sort of proclamation of the profound truth mentioned above; that the Faith belongs to the heights and the open
spaces, and the circle of the whole world, and is *not* the one thing
which its enemies go on desperately calling it; a conspiracy. There
could not be a better way of suggesting the very reverse of that
suggestion, than by the continual use in public buildings of what is

---

[85] *Quicquid agunt homines* is Latin for "Whatever men do."

large in design and hospitable in gesture. Art, and especially architecture, can here express actualities that are at once too large and
too elusive to be expressed in words. St. Mark's Cathedral at Venice
is in some ways a very curious building, and to some northern eyes
does not look like a cathedral at all; but it does look like a thing
coloured with the sunrise and the sunset, in touch with the very
ends of the earth; open like a harbour and full of popular poetry
like a fairy-palace. That is, it does express the first essential fact that
Catholicism is not a narrow thing; that it knows more than the world
knows about the potentialities and creative possibilities of the world,
and that it will outlast all the worldly and temporary expressions of
the same culture. Christianity has gone northward and established
richer ports in colder seas; it has been changed and chilled for a
time by colder heresies; but the same principle still stands for its
expansion and exaltation; that which is expressed in the expansion
and exaltation of great buildings; in the breadth of great gates declaring the brotherhood of men or the lifting of great domes pointing
the way of their destiny. To-day another such building is being reared
in what Mr. Belloc's fantasy once called a Harbour in the North;
and its scope and scale would indeed be idle things; if they did not
remind us of the two essential truths: first, that even within the world
the boundaries of the Faith are being enlarged; and second, and
much more important, that the Faith itself enlarges the world; which
would be a small thing without it.

BACK IN THE FOG

The dome of sky above Dublin was clear with the awful clarity of a burning-glass, and such a glaring gap or rent in the grey skies of Ireland was itself a portent, with some savour of a miracle. But though it was very rare in the Dublin climate, it was curiously representative of the Dublin mentality. It was none the less Irish weather because it is almost unknown in Ireland. It corresponded to the Irish brilliancy of intercourse; to the continual blend of lucidity and levity. And it was all the more Irish because there was, as there always is, in the intensity of summer, a faint thrill of thunder. It was as if the very light were lightning, and shone between two storms.

And I, who love both countries, but my own best and with most anxiety, could not help saying to myself, "This is always the real Dublin daylight. And the moment I return home, I shall find myself in the London fog."

The difference is indescribable; but that is the nearest description. There is more hatred in Dublin; and yet there is a harder sense of the obligation of justice. There is even more slander in Dublin; and yet in some strange way there is more truth. What there is in London is something that is not so much falsehood as falsification; and not so much falsification as simply fog. After a week in Ireland, the newspaper politics of England seem to be like a vast vapour, inhabited only by phantoms. There is no question of hating men or slandering men; for they are not the same men for ten weeks together; and they are never the real men at all. I will take two examples; the two men who happened to be the heads of the two Parliamentary systems of the two countries at that moment. I will not take the case of Jim Thomas; because it is beneath the seriousness of this subject. Jim Thomas is a joke; and I am sorry to say that the joke is against us. He is not a person in the same historical world as de Valera,[86] even as seen by those who hate de

[86] Eamon de Valera (1882–1975) led a party of insurgents in the 1916 Irish national uprising. He was the president of Sinn Fein (1918–1926) and of the provisional Irish government (1918–1922). He led the opposition to the Anglo-Irish treaty (1921) and was imprisoned by the Irish Free State in 1923.

Valera, of whom there are probably more in Ireland than in England. But I will take the relatively dignified figure of Mr. Thomas's revered leader; and point out as respectfully as possible that he is a ghost. He is an apparition. He is not really there. At least the figure that is recognised is not really there. Londoners live in a fog of journalism, out of which there looms from time to time a figure, who strikes certain spectral attitudes, and then vanishes in the fog and is forgotten. Not many years ago we saw start out of the mist, like the pale face of a fiend, the face of a traitor. He was reeling and ragged as if torn by patriot mobs; a golf-club was broken in his hand; as if it had been broken across his head, when he was expelled for treason from his club of fashionable golfers. He had been detected in a dastardly effort to escape to Stockholm and make a treacherous peace, and was only frustrated by the gallantry of our British tars. He was the wildest ruffian of the I.L.P.[87] and wore a red tie, which had certainly been sent to him secretly from Moscow. Well, this person, after throwing himself into a few bodily postures expressive of moral baseness and political perfidy, vanished in the fog and was never seen again. This was the infamous James Ramsay MacDonald, of atrocious memory. Only, as it happens there has been a slight lapse in the memory. The crowd waiting in the fog, however, has had other diversions. There even burst upon it just recently a beautiful and ennobling vision: a stately and handsome presence, clad almost entirely in Union Jacks, with a few patches of tartan, and wearing the ancient Civic Crown; *ob cives servatos*: the Saviour of the State. For this being was indeed that noble statesman who became the head of the National Government, sacrificing Party to Patriotism, and triumphantly routing the traitor Henderson.[88] This was the heroic James Ramsay MacDonald, of immortal memory, so long as he is remembered. There had once been another person called Henderson who had been a Patriot; when the other person called MacDonald was a Traitor; but neither of these persons could possibly be remembered.

[87] The I.L.P. was the Independent Labour party, a socialist organization established in Great Britain in 1893 under the leadership of Keir Hardy.

[88] Arthur Henderson (1863–1935) was a British labor leader and politician who at the outbreak of World War I was instrumental in influencing most of the Labour party to support the government's war policy.

Perhaps it is quite right that they should none of them be remembered; for none of them ever really existed at all. There never was any traitor named MacDonald who betrayed his country to its enemies, any more than there ever was any patriot called MacDonald who preferred his country to his party. All these shadows in the shadow-pantomime of London politics have no reference to the respectable, rather vain, very serious, self-respecting "Scotsman on the make" who has risen in the profession of politics rather less scandalously than most. That is what I mean by the London fog, and that is what I mean by the Dublin daylight.

In Dublin there are men who would kill de Valera; and there are men who would die for de Valera. But there are no men who do not know the main facts for or against him. That he is not a native Irishman, in the normal sense; that he came from America, is admitted as much by his friends as his foes. It had to be, in Ireland; for there the family is everything; and a man could not even announce himself as Mr. Brown, without provoking the most sweeping generalisations about the Browns. That he helped the guerilla war which some would call the murder of English soldiers is, of course, a matter of pride and not of apology; but at least it is not a matter of mystification. That he was anti-clerical, in the sense that the bishops and priests mostly opposed his irreconcilable indignation, is known to everybody; even to the clerics or clericals who may afterwards come to support him. There is nobody in Dublin who does not know the *story* of de Valera; and there is next to nobody in London who does know the *story* of MacDonald. That is what I mean by the London Fog.

THE HISTORIC MOMENT*

The Eucharistic Congress in Dublin has one aspect which most Englishmen will almost certainly miss altogether. It is not the Irish aspect. The English have thought too much of Ireland, even when they thought too little for Ireland; or thought only against Ireland. When debaters are informed that they must not debate on politics or religion, the more spirited and intelligent naturally retort that there is nothing else to debate about. And yet there is a third thing, which is not identical with the debate about politics and religion in Ireland, which has filled all the debating-clubs of England. That third thing is History; and it sums up the whole problem to say that the average Englishman will hardly know what is meant by mentioning it.

The average Englishman once had a hearty and even heroic hatred of the Roman Catholic religion; it has long since turned into something much milder and more tolerant. It has slowly broadened down, if not from precedent to precedent, at least from prejudice to prejudice. At worst a morbid and malignant curiosity has been replaced by a more Christian condition of ignorance. But the point is that the religious hostility has been softened; and that the special political hostility has been softened too. The average Englishman once had a passionate patriotic distrust of the political Irish; he regarded their hope of national self-expression as a mere mad mutinous breaking up of his own Empire. That also has since turned into something much milder and more tolerant. The average Englishman probably does not understand the Irish any better, if so well, as in the time of Gladstone and Parnell;[89] but he is much less disposed to punish them for being different. The Englishman no longer execrates Mr. Gladstone; he is not very likely to attend the anniversary

*Written at the Eucharistic Congress in Dublin.
[89] Charles Stewart Parnell (1846–1891) was a proponent of home rule for Ireland; in the 1880s he convinced Gladstone to support the measure.

celebration of the Boyne;[90] and is the less anxious to incur the curse of Cromwell, because he has lately begun rather to curse the Puritans himself. But there is one thought that will hardly cross his mind. And that is—how very small a part of History is that which divides us from Gladstone, or from William of Orange, or even from Oliver Cromwell.

Ages before Englishmen had any notion of being Protestants, ages before Irishmen had any need to be Nationalists, there moved across the world the great searchlights of Rome; the omnipresence of those historic and hieratic things now enthroned on their two thousand years. What corresponds to the Congress is the Council; that ancient assembly of Christendom which shifted so swiftly from Athens to Spain, or from Arabia to Gaul. Any man whose mind has been magnified by History, the greatest of all the works of the imagination, can feel the futility of allowing lesser and later quarrels entirely to obliterate the memory of that marching capital; the winged and Flying City. Wherever was that presence there was Rome; Rome was set up in the sands of the African desert; Rome in the rocky plains about Toledo. And but a few years ago, Rome was in Australia, a raw and remote colony under the Southern Cross; and to-day Rome is in Ireland, the most ancient of the Celtic cultural countries of the West. That presence was already old when Ireland civilised stood up and taught England barbarous; or rather taught something still too barbarous to be called England. It was already old when England converted Germany; when St. Boniface[91] went forth from among our own people, to baptize the barbarians of the Rhine. It is this sense of the grandeur of the great distances of human history, and the huge changes they have made between nation and nation, that is the true manner of assuaging and healing the tribal quarrels of men.

It is Ancient History that will unite the nations. It is certainly not Modern History; which has only managed to divide them. It is, least of all, Future History, of which nobody knows anything at all;

[90] Boyne was a battle in Ireland in 1690 in which the army of King William III defeated the forces supporting the deposed James II.

[91] St. Boniface (680–755) was an English missionary to the pagan Germanic tribes.

which is described in a series of Utopias discarded in turn by the Utopians. The best hope for the relations of England and Ireland is that they should both acknowledge the human authority of history; and the fact which is a fact, whether we call it Europe or Christendom. The difficulty of the English is to understand that they come out of the old religion. The difficulty of the Irish is to understand that they come out of the old civilisation. Ireland was Roman in religion but never Roman in rule. England was always Roman in rule and suddenly ceased to be Roman in religion. The essential for both is to find something deep and distant enough to be shared without the exasperation of recent political memories.

To say that new things like wireless and aviation have united nations is simply false. England and Ireland are only two out of many now much more divided. It is not new but old things that unify mankind; it is at the back of history that we rediscover humanity; it is quite strictly, in Genesis or the beginnings that we find the brotherhood of men; even if some controversy continues about which was Abel or Cain.

MARY AND THE CONVERT

I was brought up in a part of the Protestant world which can best be described by saying that it referred to the Blessed Virgin as the Madonna. Sometimes it referred to her as *a* Madonna; from a general memory of Italian pictures. It was not a bigoted or uneducated world; it did not regard all Madonnas as idols or all Italians as Dagoes. But it had selected this expression, by the English instinct for compromise, so as to avoid both reverence and irreverence. It was, when we came to think about it, a very curious expression. It amounted to saying that a Protestant must not call Mary "Our Lady," but he may call her "My Lady." This would seem, in the abstract, to indicate an even more intimate and mystical familiarity than the Catholic devotion. But I need not say that it was not so. It was not untouched by that queer Victorian evasion; of translating dangerous or improper words into foreign languages. But it was also not untouched by a certain sincere though vague respect for the part that Madonnas had played, in the actual cultural and artistic history of our civilisation. Certainly the ordinary reasonably reverent Englishman would never have intended to be disrespectful to that tradition in that aspect; even when he was much less liberal, travelled and well-read than were my own parents. Certainly, on the other hand, he was entirely unaware that he was saying "My Lady"; and if you had pointed out to him that, in fact, he was generally saying "a My Lady," or "the My Lady," he would have agreed that it was rather odd.

I do not forget, and indeed it would be a very thankless thing in me to forget, that I was lucky in this relative reasonableness and moderation of my own family and friends; and that there is a whole Protestant world that would consider such moderation a very poor-spirited sort of Protestantism. That strange mania against Mariolatry; that mad vigilance that watches for the first faint signs of the cult of Mary as for the spots of a plague; that apparently presumes her to be perpetually and secretly encroaching upon the prerogatives of Christ; that logically infers from a mere glimpse of the blue robe the presence of the Scarlet Woman—all that I have never felt or known or understood, even as a child; nor did those who had the care of my childhood. They knew nothing to speak of about the Catholic Church; they certainly did not know that anybody connected with them was ever likely to belong to it; but they did know that noble and beautiful ideas had been presented to the world under the form of this sacred figure, as under that of the Greek gods or heroes. But, while putting aside all pretence that this Protestant atmosphere was actively an anti-Catholic atmosphere, I may still say that my personal case was a little curious.

I have here rashly undertaken to write on a subject at once intimate and daring; a subject which ought indeed, by its own majesty, to make it impossible to be egotistical; but which does also make it impossible to be anything but personal. "Mary and the Convert" is the most personal of topics, because conversion is something more personal and less corporate than communion; and involves isolated feelings as an introduction to collective feelings. But also because the cult of Mary is in a rather peculiar sense a personal cult; over and above that greater sense that must always attach to the worship of a personal God. God is God, Maker of all things visible and invisible; the Mother of God is in a rather special sense connected with things visible; since she is of this earth, and through her bodily being God was revealed to the senses. In the presence of God, we must remember what is invisible, even in the sense of what is merely intellectual; the abstractions and the absolute laws of thought; the love of truth, and the respect for right reason and honourable logic in things, which God himself has respected. For, as St. Thomas Aquinas insists, God himself does not contradict the law of contradiction. But Our Lady, reminding us especially of God Incarnate, does in some degree gather up and embody all those elements of the heart and the higher instincts, which are the legitimate short cuts to the love of God. Dealing with those personal feelings, even in this rude and curt outline, is therefore very far from easy. I hope I shall not be misunderstood if the example I take is merely personal; since it is this particular part of religion that really cannot be impersonal. It may be an accident, or a highly unmerited favour of heaven, but anyhow it is a

fact; that I always had a curious longing for the remains of this particular tradition, even in a world where it was regarded as a legend.
I was not only haunted by the idea while still stuck in the ordinary
stage of schoolboy scepticism; I was affected by it before that, before
I had shed the ordinary nursery religion in which the Mother of
God had no fit or adequate place. I found not long ago, scrawled in
very bad handwriting, screeds of an exceedingly bad imitation of
Swinburne, which was, nevertheless, apparently addressed to what I
should have called a picture of the Madonna. And I can distinctly
remember reciting the lines of the "Hymn To Proserpine," out of
pleasure in their roll and resonance; but deliberately directing them
away from Swinburne's intention, and supposing them addressed to
the new Christian Queen of life, rather than to the fallen Pagan
queen of death.

> "But I turn to her still; having seen she shall surely abide in the end;
> Goddess and maiden and queen, be near me now and befriend."

And I had obscurely, from that time onwards, the very vague but
slowly clarifying idea of defending all that Constantine had set up,
just as Swinburne's Pagan had defended all he had thrown down.

It may still be noted that the unconverted world, Puritan or Pagan,
but perhaps especially when it is Puritan, has a very strange notion
of the collective unity of Catholic things or thoughts. Its exponents,
even when not in any rabid sense enemies, give the most curious
lists of things which they think make up the Catholic life; an odd
assortment of objects, such as candles, rosaries, incense (they are
always intensely impressed with the enormous importance and necessity of incense), vestments, pointed windows, and then all sorts of
essentials or unessentials thrown in in any sort of order; fasts, relics,
penances or the Pope. But even in their bewilderment, they do bear
witness to a need which is not so nonsensical as their attempts to
fulfil it; the need of somehow summing up "all that sort of thing,"
which does really describe Catholicism and nothing else except
Catholicism. It should of course be described from within, by the
definition and development of its theological first principles; but that
is not the sort of need I am talking about. I mean that men need an

image, single, coloured and clear in outline, an image to be called up instantly in the imagination, when what is Catholic is to be distinguished from what claims to be Christian or even what in one sense is Christian. Now I can scarcely remember a time when the image of Our Lady did not stand up in my mind quite definitely, at the mention or the thought of all these things. I was quite distant from these things, and then doubtful about these things; and then disputing with the world for them, and with myself against them; for that is the condition before conversion. But whether the figure was distant, or was dark and mysterious, or was a scandal to my contemporaries, or was a challenge to myself—I never doubted that this figure was the figure of the Faith; that she embodied, as a complete human being still only human, all that this Thing had to say to humanity. The instant I remembered the Catholic Church, I remembered her; when I tried to forget the Catholic Church, I tried to forget her; when I finally saw what was nobler than my fate, the freest and the hardest of all my acts of freedom, it was in front of a gilded and very gaudy little image of her in the port of Brindisi, that I promised the thing that I would do, if I returned to my own land.

A CENTURY OF EMANCIPATION

When we really wish to know how the world is going, it is no bad test to take some tag or current phrase of the press and reverse it, substituting the precise contrary, and see whether it makes more sense that way. It generally does; such a mass of outworn conventions has our daily commentary become. An excellent example occurred recently concerning the prospects of Protestantism and Catholicism. The editor of the *Sunday Express*, once better known as a sympathetic critic of letters, summed up the matter by saying that he had no prejudice against Catholicism or Anglo-Catholicism, that he had every respect for them, but that England (evidently including himself) was solidly Protestant. This is a very neat and convenient statement of the exact opposite of the truth. I have most friendly feelings to the gentleman in question; and it is without the least animosity to him that I say that what is sincere and alive and active in him is Anti-Catholicism and nothing else. What is really working in the world to-day is Anti-Catholicism and nothing else. It certainly is not Protestantism; not half so much as it is Pelagianism. And if the religion of modern England is to be called Protestant, there is at least one other adjective which cannot conceivably be applied to it. Whatever else it is, it is not solid Protestantism. There might perhaps be a case for calling it liquid Protestantism.

Now this marks the chief change of the century since Catholic Emancipation.[92] The political circumstances of the final Tory surrender to Emancipation were, of course, complex. Emancipation seemed to some a sort of mongrel and monster; produced by two opposites; the survival of the Old Religion and the principles of the French Revolution. But in such things there are complex harmonies as well as contradictions. In some ways the ultimate quarrel of Rome with the French Revolution was rather like the recent quarrel of Rome with the French Royalists. It was resistance to a pagan extreme;

[92] By a parliamentary act of 1829, Catholics in Great Britain gained full political and civil rights.

but there had been not a little Catholic sympathy before the thing reached that extreme. There had been countless liberal clerics in the first movements of the reform; Pius IX[93] had begun by being the reverse of reactionary; and the atmosphere was such that the gigantic protagonist of Catholic Emancipation himself, the great Daniel O'Connell,[94] could combine passionate Ultramontanism with the largest political Liberalism without any division in the simplicity of his mind or the general humanity of his ideals. Those who hated him both as a Radical and a Roman Catholic would have seen no inconsistency in those two hated things. The truth to seize about all that earlier situation is that the bigotry was on the other side; in one sense the theology was on the other side. We cannot see it clearly in the statesmen; for they were either freethinkers or opportunists. Wellington[95] met his Waterloo; but he was a good soldier and therefore retreated when it was futile to stand. But if we look at the mass of the people, we find a real religious resistance—because there was a real religion. That resistance is now only found in America where just such a Democrat[96] as Daniel O'Connell is still threatened with political exclusion solely for being a Catholic. In some points the Americans are a hundred years behind the times.

But this sort of purely political exclusiveness will not be the chief problem of the future. Whatever be the relation of Rome to the new world, her authority will not be transferred to Dayton, Tennessee. The political effects of the political emancipation are relatively simple and in a sense the easiest part of the speculation. Everybody knows that Catholic Emancipation has never led, and will never lead, to the direct political disasters that some foretold.

---

[93] Pius IX, who reigned from 1846 to 1878, is one of the most famous of modern popes. He proclaimed the dogma of the Immaculate Conception, issued the Syllabus of Errors and called the First Vatican Council, which declared papal infallibility in matters of faith and doctrine.

[94] Daniel O'Connell (1755–1847) was an Irish political leader.

[95] The Duke of Wellington, prime minister in 1829, opposed Catholic emancipation, but, for fear of civil war in Ireland, he pushed the bill through Parliament.

[96] In 1928 Al Smith was defeated in his bid for the presidency, in part because of opposition to his Catholicism.

The Duke of Norfolk was never actually caught in the act of imitating Guy Fawkes;[97] and Lord Russell of Killowen[98] seldom if ever invited a Spanish Armada to these shores. Outside certain local Puritan fevers, chiefly in America, there is no reason to suppose that the world will be so unreasonable as to repent having elected Catholic Mayors or sent out Catholic Ambassadors. The cant about a foreign allegiance is still heard; but that is because a cant can long outlive a cause. Men who are wide awake are well aware that the Catholic internationalism, which bids men respect their national governments, is considerably less dangerous than the financial internationalism which may make a man betray his country, or the revolutionary internationalism which may make him destroy it. It is, of course, possible that, under the pressure of Catholic conversions, the world may return to older and rougher types of persecution; but it is not immediately probable. But when we turn from the political to the spiritual prospect, we find a change which is exactly represented by the reversal of the journalistic maxim mentioned above. We must realise what England has become, under all titles and terminology, if we would make a guess about what she is next destined to be.

If we want to measure the distance between the date of emancipation and the day in which we live, between Catholic Emancipation and its consequences after a century, we shall find this newspaper quotation very important. If we want to describe the conditions a hundred years ago in this country, we could not do it better than by saying that *then* England was solidly Protestant; or the Protestantism of England was solid. And we shall still better understand the modern change, if we ask what is meant by that solidarity. It had a very definite meaning, which has now so completely disappeared that even those who most frequently invoke it are least able to imagine it. There is nothing like that sort of solid confidence to-day. It meant this: that the types and ranks of society really and sincerely interested

[97] Henry Fitzalan-Howard, Duke of Norfolk (1847–1917) was an English Catholic prominent in public life. Guy Fawkes was a participant in the alleged Catholic plot of 1605 to blow up the House of Parliament.

[98] Charles Russell, Baron Russell of Killowen (1832–1900), was Lord Chief Justice of England from 1894 to 1900.

in religion did really and sincerely believe that Protestant religion
had been proved superior to Catholic religion. It was strongest in
the middle class, especially the wealthier middle class; but that middle class had been steadily growing stronger and wealthier, as was
natural in a specially mercantile and capitalist community. It covered
a multitude of healthy, hard-headed and even clear-headed professional and commercial men; I say "even clear-headed" because, though
the English had the name of not being logical, they were far more
logical in those days than they are now. If they sat longer over their
wine, they argued longer over their politics; they did not live on
hurried cocktails and hurried headlines. Their mercantile politics
might be narrow; but the number of them who could expound some
connected thesis, such as Free Trade, was very large. And as their
politics consisted of certain definite theories, right or wrong, so their
religion consisted of certain definite doctrines, true or false. If you
had asked any such Protestant why he was a Protestant, or what he
meant by being a Protestant, he would have instantly stated or
explained those doctrines; just as a Free Trader would explain Free
Trade. There were Englishmen, of course, for whom the whole business was vaguer or more indifferent; but they did not make the tone
of that solid mercantile England. The populace made the Pope a
guy, just as they made Guy Fawkes a guy; but the poor were at the
best treated like children and left, like children, to make a guy or a
game of anything. A great part of the higher aristocracy had been
quite sceptical and pagan throughout the eighteenth century, or even
from the seventeenth century; but the same tact and informal secrecy,
which keeps such a class together, kept it from any public insult to
the Protestant religion of England. And that religion was a religion;
it was Protestant, and it was national; that is, it was the religion of
the nomal citizen.

Now if you had asked an educated English Protestant in 1828
why Protestantism was right, or why Popery was wrong, he would
not have had the smallest difficulty in answering. Of course the first
thing to be emphasised would have been what has since been the
first thing to be doubted or denied. It was the literal inspiration and
inerrancy of the Hebrew Scriptures, and sometimes even of the English

translation of those Scriptures. It was the view that still lingers in provincial corners and is called Fundamentalism.

At the beginning of the nineteenth century, practically all Protestantism was Fundamentalism. But it is a great mistake to suppose that the true Protestant of history had nothing better to do for men than to throw a Bible at their heads. What he valued was the theological Scheme of Salvation supposed to be set forth in that work; as the Free Trader valued Adam Smith as the instrument of a theory. Of that theological theory there were two main versions; one, universal in Scotland and very prevalent in England, that God chose some to receive the benefits of redemption and rejected others even in the act of creating them; the other, that men could accept God but only by accepting this theological scheme of salvation, and that their good works had no effect on the result. This was the great doctrine of Faith independent of Works, which was so universally recognised as the chief mark and test of Protestantism that we might almost say that it was the whole of Protestantism, except indeed where Protestantism took the very fiercest form of Calvinism. It is not a question of making points against Protestantism; this was the chief point that could be made for Protestantism. It was especially the popular point; the most persuasive point, the most sympathetic point. From this idea of instantaneous individualist acceptance of the Atonement, by a pure act of faith, came the whole system of appeals on which this form of Christianity relied. That was why it was so easy, so personal, so emotional; that was why the *whole* of Christian's burden fell off at the foot of the Cross. There were no degrees of sin or details of penance; because works were not in question at all. That is why they needed no Confessor or Sacrament of Penance; because there was nothing *they* could do to diminish sins either hopeless or already abolished or ignored. That was why it was wicked to pray for the dead; for the dead could not be anything but instantly beatified by dogmatic faith alone, or lost for lack of it. That was why there could be no progress of further enlightenment in the life to come; or, in other words, no Purgatory. And *that* was what was meant by being a Protestant; disapproving of prayers for the dead, disapproving of progress after death; disapproving of any religion that relied on good works. That was the great Protestant religion of Western Europe, of which we would speak as respectfully as we would of the virility and equality of Islam; and a hundred years ago it was normal and national. It was, in the newspaper phrase, solid.

To-day, as a national and normal thing, it has utterly vanished. Not one man in ninety really disapproves of praying for the dead. The War, in killing many million men, killed that pedantry and perversity. Not one man in ninety is either a Calvinist or an upholder of Faith against Works. Not one man in ninety thinks he will go to hell if he does not instantly accept the theological theory of redemption; perhaps it would be better if he did. Not one man in ninety believes the Bible infallible, as real Protestants believed it infallible. Of all that wonderful system of religious thought, thundered against Rome in so many sermons, argued against Rome in so many pamphlets, thrown out scornfully against Rome in so many Exeter Hall[99] meetings and Parliamentary debates, nothing remains. Of all that, as it affects the forward movement of the educated classes, and the future of the world, nothing remains.

But there is something that remains. Anti-Catholicism remains; though it is no longer Protestantism, any more than it is Albigensianism or Donatism.[100] And that is the factor we must grasp and estimate, if we are to estimate the outlook to-day. Protestantism is now only a name; but it is a name that can be used to cover any or every "ism" except Catholicism. It is now a vessel or receptacle into which can be poured all the thousand things that for a thousand reasons react against Rome; but it can only be full of these things because it is now hollow; because it is itself empty. Every sort of

[99] Exeter Hall was a meeting and concert hall that opened in London in 1831. It became the headquarters for the Young Men's Christian Association, from which the name derived its evangelical connotations.

[100] Albigensianism was a form of Manichaean dualism that arose in southern France in the late twelfth century. In 1208 Pope Innocent III called for a crusade to stamp out the heresy; the orthodox forces prevailed by the 1220s. Donatism was a Christian heresy of the fourth and fifth centuries that contended that an unworthy priest could not perform valid sacraments.

negation, every sort of new religion, every sort of moral revolt or
intellectual irritation, that can make a man resist the claim of the
Catholic Faith, is here gathered into a heap and covered with a convenient but quite antiquated label. When the journalists say that there
is solid Protestantism, all they mean is that there is a pretty heavy
reluctance or resistance in the matter of any return of the English to
their ancient religion; and this, up to a point, may be quite true.
But the heap is a hotch-potch; the resistance is not a rational resistance, in the sense of having a clear and commonly accepted reason;
and in so far as it has a prevailing colour, it is quite the contrary
colour to that which prevailed in Protestantism. It is even more against
Calvinism than against Catholicism; it is even more insistent on works
than were the Catholics; it would make a future life far less final and
more purely progressive than did the Catholic doctrine of Purgatory; it would make the Bible far less important than it is to a Catholic. On every single point on which the Protestant attacked the
Pope, he would now say that the modern spirit was a mere exag-
geration of the Popish errors. In so far as there is such a vague modern spirit, common to all these things, a spirit that may be called
either liberality or laxity, it never was at any time the spirit of Protestantism. It came from the Revolution and the Romantic Movement, indirectly perhaps from the Renaissance of men like Rabelais
and Montaigne; and ultimately much more from men like More and
Erasmus than from men like Calvin and Knox. When the Protestant
orators in the present crisis repeat rather monotonously, "We will
not lose the freedom we gained four hundred years ago," they show
how little they share the religion they defend. Men gained no freedom four hundred years ago; there was no particular freedom about
creating the Scottish Sabbath or preaching nothing but Predestina-
tion or even yielding to the Tudor Terror or the Cromwellian Terror.[101] But it is arguable that they gained freedom a hundred years
ago, as Catholics gained it a hundred years ago. It is tenable that

---

[101] The Tudor Terror was Queen Elizabeth's persecution of English Catholics in
the late sixteenth century. The Cromwellian Terror was Oliver Cromwell's invasion
of Ireland, from 1649 to 1652.

such freedom was the expanding effect of the American and French Revolutions and the democratic idealism which came with the nineteenth century and seems in some danger of declining with the twentieth. Above all, it is arguable that they have a certain kind of freedom *now*; not because they are Protestants, for they are not; but because they are anything they like and nothing if they like that better; because they are theists, theosophists,[102] materialists, monists or mystics on their own. How much such freedom is worth, or how much chance it has of bearing any fruit in anything positive or creative, is another matter; but in order to anticipate the next phase, it is necessary to realise that this phase is one of negative liberty, not to say anarchy. Whatever it is, it is not Protestantism; and whatever it is, it is not solid.

This is the truth symbolised in the remark on the Prayer-Book Debate; that a crowd of Free-Thinkers and Nonconformists and people of any opinions dictated the affairs of the Church of England. I am very proud of the fact that Catholics abstained from doing so and avoided a very obvious piece of bad taste. But the fact itself contains fine shades that have hardly been noticed. It is not sufficiently realised that even a congregation at the City Temple, or a crowd hearing a Dean or Canon in St. Paul's Cathedral, is often in fact almost as mixed and dubious in religion as the members of the House of Commons. Many Nonconformists are not conforming to Nonconformity; and a churchman often means only a man who never goes to chapel. Such differences exist in the same sect or even in the same man. If we would grasp the modern problem, we must simply take at random some fairly typical Englishman and note how little he really *is* anything. He has, let us say, been brought up a Congregationalist and drifted away; he is by normal and rather negative habit an Anglican; he has become by unanswered doubts and vague popular science an Agnostic; he has often wondered if there is anything in being a Theosophist; he has attended one or two séances and might be persuaded to be a Spiritualist. *That* is the man we have

---

[102] Theosophy, a syncretistic faith that combined elements from Christianity and various Asian religions, was founded in New York City in 1875 by Helena Blavatsky.

got to deal with; and not some rigid Protestant labelled Methodist or even some rigid Atheist labelled Materialist. It is that man whom we have to set out to convert, after a hundred years of relative political liberty have left the old Protestant England far behind us and the new Catholic England still far away.

It is only fair to say, of course, that events have falsified almost as much the prophecies of those who promoted Catholic Emancipation as of those who resisted it. Many Liberals hardly disguised the idea that to emancipate Catholicism would be to extinguish Catholicism. Many thought they were tolerating a dying superstition; some thought they were killing it. It is the other superstition that has been killed. But there are always new superstitions; or, to put it more moderately, new religions. And a general estimate of the chances will see them chiefly affected, I think, by the presence of these new religions side by side with that very ancient thing called Agnosticism. The real interest of the speculation is in the question of which of the two will turn out to be the really formidable opponent of the Faith in the future.

We know what is really meant by saying that the Church is merely conservative and the modern world progressive. It means that the Church is always continuous and the heresies always contradictory. We have already noted it in the case of Protestantism; and the men who now completely contradict Protestantism, even in order to contradict Catholicism. But one effect of this contrast between continuity and bewildering variety is that the Church is generally seen in the light of the last heresy. The Church is supposed to consist chiefly of the things of which that heresy happens to disapprove. So much of the Protestant tradition still remains that a great many people suppose that the chief marks of Catholicity are those which stood out as stains in the eyes of the last school of critics. Romanism is supposed to be made up of Popery and Purgatory and the Confessional, with the queerest things thrown in, such as incense and rosaries and the images of saints. But these were often the things most important to Protestants, not most important to Catholics; and not most important to the other opponents of Catholics. A Mahommedan would not connect Rome with Purgatory, because he himself believes in Purgatory; a Buddhist would not connect her with images, because he himself has images; an old pagan would not have been horrified at incense, because he used it himself. In the same way the new religions will not attack the old religion for the old reasons. A Christian Scientist will not assume that all stories of miraculous healing must have been frauds. A Spiritualist will not assume that all supernatural messages received through men must be impossible. It will be an entirely new list of charges or challenges that will come from the new mystics, who have imitated so many of the old marvels. In so far as the new religions become the leaders of the opposition, a new class of controversies will arise; with the faith-healers, for instance, upon the mystery of matter; with the psychic investigators upon the influences of evil. All this will bring us further and further from the special Protestant problems; and a hundred years hence the Church may look to her enemies something utterly different from what she looked like a hundred years ago. She will look different because she will be the same.

But if no new religion becomes important enough to be the main issue, the immediate change will be much simpler. The two centuries will probably have completed the full transition from Protestantism to Paganism. The Church will be facing once more her first and her most formidable enemy; a thing more attractive because more human than any of the heresies. This condition that can only be called Paganism is not easily defined and has often been misrepresented. In one aspect, it may be called practical materialism without the narrowness of theoretical materialism. The Pagan looks for his pleasures to the natural forces of this world; but he does not insist so strictly upon dry negations about the other; he has commonly admitted a vague borderland of the unknown, providing him with possibilities of inspiration or of awe which are forbidden to the cheap modern atheist with his clockwork cosmos. The worshippers of the Unknown God could at least build an altar, though they could not inscribe it with a name. But I fancy that men who have once been Christians, or whose fathers have been Christians, will not be long in discovering, or rather rediscovering, the profound defect that destroyed Paganism and filled centuries with a horror of its final phase. The natural forces, when they are turned into gods, betray mankind by something that is in the very nature of nature-worship. We can already see men becoming unhealthy by the worship of health; becoming hateful by the worship of love; becoming paradoxically solemn and overstrained even by the idolatry of sport; and in some cases strangely morbid and infected with horrors by the perversion of a just sympathy with animals. Unless all these things are subject to a more centralised and well-balanced conception of the universe, the local god becomes too vivid, we might say too visible, and strikes his worshippers with madness. The pantheist is always too near to the polytheist and the polytheist to the idolator; the idolator to the man offering human sacrifice. There is nothing in Paganism to check its own exaggerations; and for that reason the world will probably find again, as it found before, the necessity of a universal moral philosophy supported by an authority that can define. In any case, that quarrel between Paganism and Catholicism will again be one raising issues very unfamiliar to many even now; and issues that would have very much mystified the men who debated a hundred years ago the issue of Catholic Emancipation.

In any case, this emergence of new issues will reveal more and more one of the advantages of an old religion. Whole aspects of Catholic doctrine and tradition, hidden by historical accident and the special quarrels of recent times, will be revealed to the world when it begins to address new questions to the Church. This is a point that has not been sufficiently stressed in the relations between Protestantism and Catholicism. Very often a Protestant was not only a man merely protesting, but a man merely protesting against a particular thing. He sometimes thought that thing was Rome; but it was really only one of the thousand aspects of Rome. When new aspects appear under new searchlights, he will be not so much defeated as simply outside the affair. A Baptist disapproves of baptising babies; a Presbyterian disapproves of bishops; a Prohibitionist disapproves of beer, and so on. But a Presbyterian, as such, has nothing very special to say about the Subconscious Mind. A Baptist as such has nothing special to say to a Behaviourist as such. But a Catholic may have a great deal to say to these people. For the Catholic commentary on life has gone on so much longer, it has covered so many different social conditions, has dealt so carefully with countless fine shades of metaphysics or casuistry, that it really has a relation to almost any class of speculation that may arise. Thus, in the matter of psychoanalysis and the study of the subconscious, the Church will probably be found sooner or later defending certain essentials about Will and Conscience against a welter of wild impersonality. Catholics remembering Catholicism will have a right and reason to do this. But Calvinists who have half forgotten Calvinism have no particular reason to do it.

There is, for instance, one influence that grows stronger every day, never mentioned in the newspapers, not even intelligible to people in the newspaper frame of mind. It is the return of the Thomist Philosophy; which is the philosophy of commonsense, as compared with the paradoxes of Kant and Hegel and the Pragmatists. The Roman religion will be, in the exact sense, the only Rationalistic religion. The other religions will not be Rationalist but Relativist; declaring that the reason is itself relative and unreliable; declaring that Being is only Becoming or that all time is only a time of transition; saying in mathematics that two and two make five in the fixed stars, saying in metaphysics and in morals that there is a good beyond good and evil. Instead of the materialist who said that the soul did not exist, we shall have the new mystic who says that the body does not exist. Amid all these things the return of the Scholastic will simply be the return of the sane man. There will perhaps be belated and benighted modernists, lingering from the nineteenth century, who will repeat the jaded journalistic catchword that the Schoolman only cared to ask how many angels could stand on the point of a needle. But it will be difficult to make even that fancy appear very fantastic, in a world where men deny that it hurts a man to stick the point of the needle in his leg. If there are angels, they have presumably some intellectual relation to place and space; and if there are no angels, there are still men and presumably sane men. But to say that there is no pain, or no matter, or no evil, or no difference between man and beast, or indeed between anything and anything else—this is a desperate effort to destroy all experience and sense of reality; and men will weary of it more and more, when it has ceased to be the latest fashion; and will look once more for something that will give form to such a chaos and keep the proportions of the mind of man. Millions of men are already at least wondering whether this solution is not to be found in the Catholic order and philosophy. Above all, the Church has regained that unique position in the world in a fair field and under the very reverse of favour; having had for a hundred years no more than the common right of speaking and publishing and voting in popular assemblies; and as her Master affirmed his divinity by becoming a man among men, she has become for a season a sect among sects, to emerge at the end as something separate or supreme.

TRADE TERMS

It is grimly significant that the Organ of Empire[103] has already begun to call its Imperial policy by the cheerful name of "The Empire Merger." The sort of combine, which all free peoples have punished as a conspiracy, is now so fashionable that it is considered quite a compliment to apply this commercial term instead of a political title. Courtiers in the future, instead of saying "Your Majesty" will say "Your Monopoly"; especially when addressing Moritz IV, of the historic House of Mond,[104] by that time Emperor of the World State. But indeed we rather doubt whether there will be even so much dignity as this in such a despotism as that. The man who prefers to say, "Imperial Merger" rather than Imperial Protection or Imperial Free Trade, is already in this curious modern mood, which actually thinks mercantile terms higher than moral or social ones. The whole system of a great nation will be remodelled on the habits of a big business. The national envoy in Paris, instead of being called, "His Excellency the British Ambassador," will be called "Our Mr. Honeybubble," and he will travel with samples and be proud of being called a commercial traveller. The monopolist newspapers never weary of telling us that the world ought to have outgrown the stilted and pompous language of the old Protocols and Ultimatums, and all the formal statements of the treaties which have so often been denounced as Secret Diplomacy. Doubtless the great statesmen of the great states, the heirs of Richelieu and Canning,[105] will correspond in a brighter and brisker English, running "Yrs. rcd. and conts: noted," when indeed it is necessary to put the arrangements into writing at all. After all, it will be even more business-like to make the international arrangements in a husky and confidential voice, in the intervals of observing "What's yours?" and "Say when." That is the great

[103] The Organ of Empire was Lord Beaverbrook's *Daily Express*.

[104] Chesterton is alluding to Alfred Moritz Mond (1868–1930), an English financier and magnate in the chemical industry; he advocated industrial consolidation.

[105] George Canning (1770–1827) was a British foreign secretary in the 1820s and briefly, in 1827, prime minister.

advantage of the New Diplomacy over the old Secret Diplomacy. The old was so very secret as to write down all its secrets in laborious documents and send them round to about fifty people in Government offices. The New Diplomacy need never be written down at all; indeed, it is better not.

We are prepared, of course, to be told that all this ugly and undignified school of manners is very practical, and that the old stately or stilted school of manners was very unpractical. After all, the old theory of dignity did only trivial and incidental things, such as creating the Roman Empire, creating the French Monarchy and the French Revolution, founding the American Republic and establishing by personal adventure that very Empire, which our hustlers and hucksters can only help by impersonal advertisement. These are slight achievements compared with that of insuring that the same bad ginger-beer shall be sold everywhere, to the exclusion and extinction of good ginger-beer, or that over some thousand square miles of God's green earth nobody shall have anything but one kind of hat or one kind of house. But though these arguments are undoubtedly cogent and persuasive, and bear a certain appearance of practicality and realism, we are disposed to supplement them by a suggestion or reminder; the hint of something which even thinkers so lucid seem to have overlooked. Nowadays, it is considered very horrible to mention it; and it is indeed very horrible to test it or experience it. Nevertheless, it is a thing that may be tested or experienced; and, even to be avoided, had much better be mentioned.

Authority ruling men must be respected; it must even be loved. Men must in the last resort love it; for the simple reason that men must in the last resort die for it. No community or constitution can survive and retain its identity at all, that has not in the minds of its subjects enough of an ideal identity, to appear to them in certain extremes of peril as the vision of something to be saved. It is on that ideal, inhering in the reality, that every state will depend when there is a struggle of life and death. Men must feel something more about England than that she is commercial, something more about France than that Frenchmen are practical and careful about money, something more about America than that she happens at the moment to be monstrously rich,* before any healthy and humorous human being will kill somebody else or be killed himself, and go out from the sunlight and the sane loves of this world, for the sake of any such abstraction. It will be found, therefore, that the practical theory fails at the most practical moment. It is useful while there is question of whether the commonwealth shall continue to be rich, or continue to be imperial, or continue to be monopolist. It is useless when there is question of whether the commonwealth shall continue to be. The materialistic state, cemented only with money as with mud, will fall apart under the blow of any people who have love or loyalty to their leaders or their cause; for the simple reason that those who care most for money care more for life. One may like or dislike the Fascism of Italy, the fiery nationalism of the Poles, the deep Catholicism of the Irish; but there is no doubt that their ideals can be idealised. They are conceptions for which real men can be worked up into a real rapture of sacrifice. The images under which they are presented to the world, and especially the world of their worshippers, the golden or the silver eagle, the breastplate of St. Patrick, the Roman salute, are things that do in fact lift up the heart, and were made by the mind so that they should uplift the heart. In short there is in them poetry; and that poetry is the most practical thing in the world.

Now if the new Imperialists insist on talking of everything in terms of the counter and the commercial room, if they insist on calling Imperial Preference a Merger, as Lord Beaverbrook[106] did, if they insist on comparing a General Election to a Company Flotation, as Mr. Amery[107] did, they will make men familiar indeed with their government, and in a sense at home with it, but no more capable of loving it than of loving any unlucky investment. The time will come when its existence will depend on its power on the imagination; and it will be dignity or death. Nor will that dignity come solely from an Imperial Isolation; which seems merely to mean, "How we may think in continents without thinking of the Continents."

---

*But easier to die for, now she is poor.

[106] William Max Aitken, Lord Beaverbrook (1879–1964), was a Canadian-born English newspaper magnate and politician.

[107] Leopold Charles Maurice Stennet Amery (1873–1955) was an English journalist and prominent figure in the Conservative party in the 1920s.

FROZEN FREE THOUGHT

I believe I am in possession of a piece of news which, as we say in Fleet Street, has a certain news-value. It is hardly fitted to be flashed along the telegraph wires or blazoned on the big posters; it does not definitely involve an individual, but rather generally a school; it is an historical event; something that has happened and has hardly been noticed among the many changes of the day. The substance of the news is this. The sort of man we once knew as a Secularist has become a religious maniac.

Of course he is not actually mad, in the medical sense; nor, for that matter, is he religious in the religious sense, or perhaps in any sense. Yet the words I have used, to cover very varying stages of the malady in a fairly loose group, are the only words that convey the sharpness and importance of the incident. I mean that the *tone* of the old Fleet Street atheism, which I knew and loved of old, has entirely altered. It has come to resemble almost exactly the tone of the Seventh Day Adventists or the Millennial Dawnists,[108] or all those queerly prosaic and even prim fanatics who wander about handing out pamphlets, crowded with texts and vivid with italics, in which a new heaven and a new earth can be made out of a neglected cloud in the Book of Daniel or an unusually Little Horn in the Apocalypse. Perhaps the shortest way of distinguishing between the two literary styles is to record that the first was readable and the second is unreadable. The old atheist arguments, inherited from Bradlaugh and Foote, were always crude and therefore a little heavy, even for any agnostic with some background of history and philosophy. But they were at least as clear as they were crude; and we should all of us have agreed that a paper like the *Freethinker* was easy to read; even if some of us would have added that it was easy to answer. The *Freethinker* as it is to-day is not easy to read. I know, because I have just been reading it. Its editor has kindly sent me a copy, containing what appears from the frequent mention of my name to be an attack

---

[108] The Millennial Dawnists were Jehovah's Witnesses.

149

on myself; and when I am thus personally addressed I think it only polite to answer. If it is now not so easy to answer, it is simply because it is now not so easy to understand. It seems to be about a book I wrote on Victorian Literature[109] several years before the War; but the Freethinkers of Fleet Street, ever on the alert for fresh developments, have pounced upon it already. I have read the critique over patiently several times, and am still somewhat puzzled by what the critic can possibly mean by some of his allusions and complaints. I remember that in that very able book *The Flight from Reason*, Mr. Arnold Lunn narrates a similar experience with the same paper. He prints the whole of the Freethinker's criticism on him, and, naturally not being able to make head or tail of it, simply leaves it to the reader in despair. It was something about how anybody, who thinks there is good historical evidence for the Resurrection, is logically bound to believe the story of Aladdin in the *Arabian Nights*. I have no idea why. But what I would first emphasise, before trying to explain my critic's remarks to myself and him, is the curious character of this change in the Secularist Press, from a tone that was crude to a tone that is really crazy.

We might take a working parallel; fortunately outside the sphere of religion. I can imagine a jolly old Radical working man talking in the old mutinous manly fashion against the King or the House of Lords, saying with surly geniality and some repetition; "What we want with a King? Why should 'e 'ave a golden crown on 'is 'ead and me only my old boko? What's 'e blasted well doing in Buckingham Palace ——" and so on. Now I like that sort of man. I like him very much. I know what he means. I think there is, in the last resort, a lot to be said for it. It is not in the style of the *De Monarchia*;[110] it hardly appreciates the subtleties of Mr. Charles Maurras. But it has truths behind it; the equality of men and something that is right in republican simplicity. But suppose that man, who begins by saying he is as good as the King, broods and eventually

[109] Chesterton is referring to *The Victorian Age in Literature* (1912).
[110] *De Monarchia* was Dante's defense, written between 1309 and 1312, of the Holy Roman Emperor's supremacy over the pope in temporal affairs.

goes mad saying that he *is* the King. Suppose his grievance becomes a personal grievance about his great-grandfather, and he goes about boring people with plans and pedigrees to prove his Plantagenet blood. We know the whole atmosphere will alter; but chiefly in clarity. Everybody knew what the grumbler meant; nobody will listen to what the lunatic means. That is very like the difference between the Old Secularist and the New Secularist or the Millennial Dawnist.

Take some puzzles out of this page about me. "Chesterton uses his talents tyrannously in the service of the most reactionary of all Churches,"—to which he didn't belong at the time. And how do you use talents tyrannously? I wish I knew. "He has nothing but the crudest insults for the great intellectuals." Well, there is the book; anybody can see what I really said about Mill, about Meredith,[111] about Matthew Arnold, about Huxley, even supposing that nobody is an intellectual unless he is an agnostic. To say I had "nothing" but crude insult for them is—well, something that could be described still more crudely. Swinburne, it seems "is accused of composing a learned and sympathetic and indecent parody on the Litany of the Blessed Virgin." And the critic adds mysteriously, "an ironical suggestion in a Protestant country." I do not know what the word "accused" means here. If the critic has read Swinburne he knows that an early verse in *Dolores* is a parody of the Litany of the Virgin. It is hardly an accusation to call it learned and sympathetic; by which I meant artistically sympathetic in an archaic Gothic mode; as were the profane Pre-Raphaelites as well as the pious ones. Whether such a thing is indecent may be discussed; but the critic is quite wrong in fancying that only Papists thought it indecent. The indecency of *Dolores* was denounced, more harshly than I dreamed of doing it, by the first Freethinker in English public life; the late John Morley.[112]

---

[111] George Meredith (1828–1909) was an English poet and novelist, best known for the novel *The Egoist* (1879).

[112] John Morley (1838–1923) was an English statesman, biographer, historian and editor.

Finally, here is one wonderful example of how the *Freethinker* gets hold of the wrong end of the stick, even when I actually offer him the right end. He writes the amazing sentence, "Even the great authors of the nineteenth century do not escape his Romish censure, and are dubbed, spitefully, 'lame giants'." It is not very spiteful to call an author a giant; but anyone consulting the book will see that the men I called "lame giants" were not "the great authors of the nineteenth century," but specially the English authors of the Victorian time; whom I compared unfavourably with the franker and bolder Freethinkers of France and the Continent. Thus I praised Renan as a more logical sceptic than Tennyson, who was a lame sceptic, hampered by respectability and provincial religion. You would think a Freethinker would recognise that as an obvious concession to Freethinkers. But the new Freethinker does not *read* a book. He looks through it feverishly for texts to be twisted in favour of a prejudice, like the religious maniac with the Bible.

To take another instance. I wrote an article, which appeared in the *London Mercury* and was called "The End of the Moderns," in which I tried to describe a certain quality in works like *Brave New World*, and in much of the cult of D. H. Lawrence; a quality (not necessarily a bad quality) of being near the end of its tether, or having nearly run through its resources: of having stretched something very nearly as far as it will go. It was a psychological and literary note upon certain literary psychologists of recent years; it had nothing directly to do with religion, still less with irreligion; it had nothing in the world to do with any attack on atheism. Now the Freethinker reads through all this stuff about Lawrence and Aldous Huxley, all terribly modern to him, of course; but the point is that he cannot believe that any article I write can be anything except an attack on atheism; and especially on his own antediluvian sort of atheism. That anybody should want to write an article about modern authors, and their psychological, sociological and ethical difficulties, he cannot conceive. Therefore he runs his eye through my article, until it brightens suddenly at the sight of the word "blasphemy". At last he has found something that he understands; something that he knows all about. Blasphemy brings back Bradlaugh and the brave days of old; and, by a pardonable optical illusion, I appear to him in the form of Lord Randolph Churchill[113] in the '80s, moving the expulsion of the Senior Member for North-ampton. I am, after all, making my unscrupulous Attack on Athe-ism, though (for some dark reasons best known to myself) I prefer to stick it into the middle of an article stuffed with all sorts of strange nonsense about literature and a man named Lawrence.

Why, and in what connection, as a matter of fact, did I use the sacred word "blasphemy?" The point was this; I wished to give the reader a rough working example, to begin with, of what I meant by saying that a literary process or argument could be doomed to an early exhaustion; could be of a kind that was fated to come to a finish. And I gave the example of the purely literary and artistic effect of blasphemy. I was careful to state, in so many words, that I was only talking of the literary and artistic effect. I said the partic-ular shock or thrill, given by breaking the silence about a sanctity, cannot be repeated indefinitely, when the sanctity is no longer there. I never said a word about whether it would be a good thing, on general social grounds, that the sanctity should be no longer there. I was not discussing that question, but another question about short-lived literary effects, of which blasphemy happens to be a good work-ing example. But the monomaniac solemnity of the Freethinker leads him to come blundering out with a very heavy club, against the blasphemer who has blasphemed the sanctity of blasphemy. He labours a ludicrous comparison, according to which saying, "there is no sense in blasphemy when there is nothing sacred to blaspheme" is no more sensible than saying "there is no sense in sanitation when there are no enemies of sanitation to attack." What has become of the rea-soning power of atheists, I cannot think. This comparison is obvi-ously rubbish; because sanitation is supposed to be useful whether it is opposed or no; and all I said was blasphemy was not startling or thrilling unless there was something to which it was opposed. Whether secularism would be a good thing, when once established and unopposed, as sanitation is supposed to be a good thing when

---

[113] Lord Randolph Churchill (1849–1895) led the fight to prevent Charles Brad-laugh from taking his seat in Parliament, unless Bradlaugh, a noted freethinker, agreed to swear his oath of office on the Bible.

established and unopposed, was a question which I simply did not raise in that particular article at all. I only said that such a settled secular state could not enjoy eternally the artistic excitement of blasphemy; and this the secularist, after beating wildly about the bush is eventually forced to admit. "What Mr. Chesterton ought to have said is that the defiance of God, the criticism of God, or ridiculing God, can only exist so long as men believe in God. That is quite true." That is also, as it happens, exactly what Mr. Chesterton said, and all that Mr. Chesterton said; and Mr. Chesterton is very much gratified to learn that it is also what he ought to have said. But Mr. Chesterton also said a lot more, on literary and psychological matters of the moment, in which he happens to be interested; and he is now mildly interested in the fact that *The Freethinker* is not in the least interested in them. The atheist is not interested in anything except attacks on atheism, so he insists that I am attacking atheism, even when I explain elaborately that I am doing something else. He therefore blames me for saying what he himself declares to be true; or for not proving what I had never set out to prove.

But the queerest thing of all is this. I was not then attacking atheism, and I was actually defending rationalism. I was doing the poor old Freethinker's job for him; and defending the Reason that he ought to defend. I was defending it against the more modern mysticism of D. H. Lawrence, who said that we should rebel *against* reason: and rely entirely upon instinct and emotion. And *this*, I pointed out, was an instance of something which, like blasphemy in literature, may be stimulating at the very start, but cannot run very long. An attempt really to conduct life, without constant reference to reason, would quite certainly break down. That was my point about all these modern social suggestions; that they would break down. For the rest, he repeats at intervals with hissing emphasis that I am a Roman Catholic; he is so much out of touch with the twentieth century that he really seems to imagine that a Roman Catholic is now at an intellectual disadvantage among other Christians. But I want to know why the Roman Catholic is left to do the work of the Rationalist; and attack the really recent upheaval of Unreason in the world, and why the Rationalist actually attacks him for attacking it.

SHOCKING THE MODERNISTS

How do we manage to stagger on blinded by the blaze of wit and starry brilliancy, that is showered upon us like everlasting fireworks every day in the daily papers? The writers in those papers who so often remind us, with never-failing freshness, that things that were once rare luxuries are now multiplied and minutely and exactly imitated everywhere, surely will not fail to apply this same striking truth to the intellectual world. They will doubtless point out that those perfect and pointed epigrams, which were once heard only from exceptional individuals, like Voltaire and Talleyrand, are now invented by the hundred in every column of every newspaper, and it is hardly possible to find a single dull sentence wedged between the witty repartees and immortal jests, which can now, like everything else of any value, be produced in any quantity by mass production.

However this may be, there can be no doubt that our journalism, and the world it describes, has reached an acute sensibility to wit and verbal brilliance, which has never been known before; and is so vividly alert and alive to any such ringing and rapier-like logical fencing as to cry "a hit! a palpable hit!" in circumstancs in which it is only too likely that our duller forefathers would have remained deaf or indifferent. I once read a paragraph in a daily paper, about a notable outburst among the most advanced intellects in the Church of England, which bears witness to the promptitude with which such triumphs are appreciated. Under the two headlines of "Youth Finds Church a Bore," and "A Girl Tells Clergy," the paragraph, or rather series of paragraphs was arranged in a suitably sensational way as follows:—

> "Youth finds church a bore—and stays away from it.
>
> This contention, put forward by a girl of eighteen from the platform at Girton College, Cambridge, yesterday, made the elderly delegates to the Modern Churchman's Conference sit up sharply in their seats.
>
> The speaker was the attractive daughter of a Portsmouth naval chaplain.

Her most telling passage was this: 'I don't think public worship has any attraction whatsoever for the young. Religion is supposed to express God through truth and beauty, we are told, but in this age of specialisation people turn to science, art and philosophy to satisfy those needs'."

I wonder what her least telling passage was.

Of course the fun really begins with the astounding and staggering effect produced by the original thunderbolt of thought "Youth Finds Church a Bore," on all those admittedly elderly delegates who were sufficiently ancient to be described as Modern Churchmen. Dr. Major[114] leapt to his feet with a howl; Dean Inge bounced up to the ceiling like a ball. Dr. Rashdall[115] uttered one piercing shriek and fainted; for not one of these venerable doctors, in all their long experience of the Modernist Movement, had ever heard one human being articulate with human lips the star-staggering blasphemy that youth finds church a bore. Not one of them had ever heard so much as a rumour of young people yawning during a sermon; to none had any voice dared to whisper that little boys have been known to catch flies or dig penknives into pews during Divine service; not one of them had ever in his life heard a baby begin to squeal in church; none had ever listened to the hideous slander that youths and maidens in church had been known to look at each other instead of keeping their eyes fixed rigidly on the lectern (for nobody in the church of a Modern Churchman would condescend to look at the altar); none of them ever knew before that there had ever been any friction between the fits and moods of youth and the routine of religion. Never, until the attractive daughter of a Portsmouth naval chaplain made this stupendous discovery in modern psychology, had they even thought of the possibility that a long religious service might be rather a bore to a boy.

[114] Henry Major (1871–1961) was one of the foremost Anglican modernist theologians. He founded the magazine *Modern Churchman* in 1911 and edited it until 1955.

[115] Hastings Rashdall (1858–1924) was an English philosopher, theologian and historian, known especially for his writings on medieval universities.

But yet, even about that discovery, it seems as if there might be more to be said. Some of the elderly Modern Churchmen have been schoolmasters. It seems just possible that some of them had discovered that the Sixth Book of the Æneid can be a bore to a boy. But in those cases it was not invariably assumed that the boy was right and the poet was wrong. It was not taken for granted that the boredom of the boy in itself proves that Virgil is a bad poet; still less did anyone ever propose that a simplified and modernised version of Virgil must be substituted for the old one. Nobody proposed that passages from Kipling about the British Empire should be substituted for the more austere salutations of Virgil to the Roman Empire, because such education would be more modern, compact and convenient to a truly National Church. Nobody proposed that a really smart and snappy up-to-date description of the Derby, taken from an evening paper, should be regarded as a complete substitute for that thundering line in which the very earth shakes with the horse-hoofs of the charioteers. And, if I may venture to hint a disagreement with the Prophetess of Girton College, Cambridge, I think it will be found that the same argument applies even to the substitutes that she herself proposes. She says that people turn to science, art and philosophy. Will she swear by the Death of Nelson, or whatever oath binds the daughter of a Portsmouth naval chaplain, that no science student ever shirks or plays truant in a science school? It will be vain for her to swear any such thing in the case of an art school; for I have been to an art school myself, and I can assure her that there were quite as many art students who found application to art a bore as there could possibly be divinity students who found divinity a bore. As for young philosophers, I have known a good many of them; at an age when nearly all of them were much more fond of philosophising than of learning philosophy. And I might hint that there are other young agitators, of the sort that seem to agitate so strangely the Modern Churchmen and the modern newspapers, who seem to have a certain spirited and spontaneous preference for saying things rather than for thinking what they are saying. Is it really necessary that we should toil through all this tiresome repetition about the perfectly obvious difficulty of getting young people to work when they naturally want to play, before we even begin to discuss the mature problem of the relation of doctrine to the mind? It is perfectly natural that the boy should find the church a bore. But why are we bound to treat what is natural as something actually superior to what is supernatural; as something which is not even merely supernatural, but is in the exact sense super-supernatural?

A GRAMMAR OF KNIGHTHOOD

I think it very likely that many have never even heard of *The Broad-stone of Honour*, the manual of chivalry written by Kenelm Digby[116] early in the nineteenth century; unless they remember one contemptuous reference to it in Macaulay's Essays. The reference is not much of a criticism on *The Broadstone of Honour*, but it is a very damaging criticism of Macaulay's Essays. It illustrates, not only his spirited superficiality, but that considerable element of ignorance that went along with his remarkable reputation for omniscience. Just as his celebrated sneer at Spenser shows that he had not read Spenser, so his less famous sneer at Kenelm Digby shows that he had not read Kenelm Digby. He set himself to belittle certain old tales of courtesy, which is the wedding of humility with dignity. He scoffed at such stories as that of the Black Prince[117] waiting like a servant on his helpless captive; and he thought he could not scoff at them more effectively than by saying they would be suitable to Kenelm Digby; or, as he put it, to "those who think, like the author of *The Broad-stone of Honour*, that God made the world for the use of gentlemen." One is tempted to reply, in some moods, that there will always be enough bounders, even among the learned, to redress the balance.

Now Kenelm Henry Digby was, as his name implies, a member of an old Catholic family, established in Ireland; and, as with the other branches of such old families established in England, it would not be very unnatural if he did attach some importance to being a gentleman. If the weakness has sometimes been too apparent in the old Catholics of England, it is at least pardonable and rather pathetic. When you are an honest and perfectly patriotic squire, and all your countrymen regard you as a liar, a traitor, a poisoner and a devil-worshipper, it must be something of a sentimental comfort to you that they cannot deny you are a gentleman. Poor human nature being

---

[116] Digby (1800–1880) published the book in 1822.

[117] The Black Prince was Prince Edward, the eldest son of King Edward III, who ruled England from 1327 to 1377.

what it is, you may be excused if you come to think a little too much of it. And Kenelm Digby might have been excused if he really had thought too much of it; and talked nonsense about gentlemen, as if God had made the world for them. But as a simple fact, it was not Digby who talked nonsense about gentlemen, but Macaulay who talked nonsense about Digby.

What would Macaulay have said if after writing his epigram about a universe created for the gentry, he had made the bold experiment of opening the book at random, as I did, and reading a paragraph like this:

"The noble Italian Arnigio shows how truly generous and heroic peasants and men of the lowest rank of life may become." "The glorious nativity of the Redeemer of the world," he observes, "was revealed to shepherds, as to men pure, just and vigilant. When our adorable Saviour was to be born blessed Mary and the devout Joseph were so little possessed of worldly grandeur that the stable of an inn was their only place of refuge. For mark, says a holy man, the evangelists do not say that there was no room in the inn, but there was no room for them. Oh what a noble school is poverty! What a temple of sovereign honour! Pope Urban IV was so little ashamed of being the son of a shoemaker that he ordered the pulpit of the church of St. Urban, at Troyes, his native city, to be adorned on great festivals with tapestry representing his father's stall. There is even an example of legislation, on the principles of the romances, which places Chivalry before nobility; for the state of Pistoja, in the thirteenth century, ennobled men as a punishment for their crimes."

Do you think that perhaps even Macaulay would have felt slightly ashamed of himself?

Anyhow, the author of *The Broadstone of Honour* did not think the world was made only for gentlemen. He thought in his simplicity that it was made for man; and he could not escape from a prejudice in favour of brave men and honest men and (I am so antiquated as to add) men who felt a special consideration for women. The book has some of the faults of its type and time; in that sense it is now rather dated; nearly as much dated as Macaulay. We must read it, or at least parts of it, rather as we read a song of Tom Moore or a patriotic poem of Thomas Davis,[118] or all that rather rhetorical yet very red-blooded tradition of talking and writing that derived from the mighty melodrama of Byron or was sympathetically satirised in Micawber.[119] But when we have allowed for variations in the taste for purple patches, a matter entirely relative in our taste as in his, the book is sustained from first to last by what can only be called a sustained energy of virtue. It does anybody good to meet a man so little ashamed of an enthusiasm for mere goodness. Many of his gestures are as noble as any of those that make the decisive moments in the Chansons de Geste.[120] Many of his concessions are as graceful as any that he himself praises in the chronicles of the tournament or the tented field. But he was very far from being merely an amiable old antiquary haunting Melrose[121] by moonlight; or even a dazed Don Quixote with his head hidden in folios about Arthur and Amadis of Gaul.[122] I cannot resist making another quotation, which will serve to show that Kenelm Digby was not by any means unconscious of what was going on in his own time—and, I will add, is still going on in ours.

After speaking of St. Francis and of many knights who would feed the poor and eat with them and carry their coffins, he says, "Oh! is it for the rich of the nineteenth century to talk of the inhumanity of the Middle Ages? To give alms, with them, is to encourage idleness. He is hungry, he is naked? Let him work. But he is old? There are employments for all. But he is a child? Do not teach him to beg. It is the mother of a large family? Perhaps she does not tell the truth. We have institutions on a new system. Yes truly, and

[118] Thomas Moore (1779–1852) was a poet whose *Irish Melodies* (1807–1835) made him Ireland's foremost lyricist. Thomas Osborne Davis (1814–1845) was an Irish nationalist and poet.

[119] Micawber is a character in Dickens' *David Copperfield*.

[120] The *Chansons de Geste* are epic poems in Old French, the earliest of which date from the twelfth century. The most famous of the *chansons*, which deal with chivalry, courtly romance and heroic exploits, is the *Song of Roland*.

[121] Melrose Abbey appears in Sir Walter Scott's poem *The Lay of the Last Minstrel* (1805).

[122] Amadis of Gaul is an eponymous protagonist of an Iberian romance written by García de Montalvo in the late fifteenth century.

woe to the unhappy ones who are doomed to receive relief from them! In order that the children of pleasure may not be incommoded by the sight of poverty the poor are shut up within high walls and condemned to confinement for the crime of being poor and miserable. When they are thus secluded from the enjoyment of nature an odious Board of Governors takes care that they should be provided with what is sufficient to support life. And then they have to endure the countenances of ferocious barbarians who are the officers to administer this horrible humanity."

That is the testimony of Digby, as it is the testimony of Dickens, who did not presumably labour under the illusion that God made the world only for gentlemen. That is also the testimony of Cobbett,[123] of Carlyle, of Hood, of Ruskin, of everybody who actually watched the modern industrial movement with his eyes open; but the fact that Digby wrote that paragraph may alone be my apology for writing this note on his neglected name.

[123] William Cobbett (1763–1835) was an English political radical and agricultural reformer, whose best-known book was *Rural Rides* (1830).

REFLECTIONS ON A ROTTEN APPLE

Our age is obviously the Nonsense Age; the wiser sort of nonsense being provided for the children and the sillier sort of nonsense for the grown-up people. The eighteenth century has been called the Age of Reason; I suppose there is no doubt that the twentieth century is the Age of Unreason. But even that is an understatement. The Age of Reason was nicknamed from a famous rationalist book.[124] But the rationalist was not really so much concerned to urge the rational against the irrational; but rather specially to urge the natural against the supernatural. But there is a degree of the unreasonable that would go even beyond the unnatural. It is not merely an incredible tale, but an inconsistent idea. As I pointed out to somebody long ago, it is one thing to believe that a beanstalk scaled the sky, and quite another to believe that fifty-seven beans make five.

For instance, a man may disbelieve in miracles; normally on some *a priori* principle of determinist thought; in some cases even on examination of the evidence. But on being told of the miracle of the multiplication of the loaves and fishes, he is told something that is logical if it is not natural. He is not told that there were fewer fishes because the fishes had been multiplied. Multiplication is still a mathematical term; and a mob all feeding on miraculous fishes is a less mysterious or monstrous sight than a man saying that multiplication is the same as subtraction. Such a story, for such a sceptic, does not carry conviction; but it does make sense. He can recognise the logical consequence, if he cannot understand the logical cause. But no pope or priest ever asked him to believe that thousands died of starvation in the desert because they were loaded with loaves and fishes. No creed or dogma ever declared that there was too little food because there was too much fish. But that is the precise, practical and prosaic definition of the present situation in the modern science of economics.

---

[124] Chesterton is referring to Thomas Paine's *The Age of Reason*, published in two parts, 1794–1795.

And the man of the Nonsense Age must bow his head and repeat his *credo*, the motto of his time, *Credo quia impossibile.*[125]

Or again, the term unreason is sometimes used rather more reasonably; for a sort of loose or elliptical statement, which is at least illogical in form. The most popular case is what was called the Irish Bull; often suspected of resembling the Papal Bull, in being a supernatural monster bred of credulity and superstition. But even this old sort of confusion stopped short of the new sort of contradiction. If any Irishman really does say, "We are not birds, to be in two places at once," at least we know what he means, even if it is not what he says. But suppose he says that one bird has been miraculously multiplied into a million birds, and that in consequence there are fewer birds in the world than there were before. We should then be dealing, not merely with an Irish Bull but with a Mad Bull, and concerned not with the incredible but with the incomprehensible. Or, to apply the parable, the Irish have sometimes been accused of unbalanced emotion or morbid sentiment. But nobody says that they merely imagined the Great Famine, in which multitudes starved because the potatoes were few and small. Only suppose an Irishman had said that they starved because the potatoes were gigantic and innumerable. I think we should not yet have heard the last of the wrongheaded absurdity of that Irishman. Yet that is an exact description of the economic condition to-day as it affects the Englishman. And, to a great extent, the American. We learn that there is a famine because there is not a scarcity; and there is such a good potato-crop that there are no potatoes. The Irishman, with his bull or his bird, is quite a hard-headed realist and rationalist compared to that. Thus, the old examples of the fantastic fell far short of the modern fact; whether they were mysteries supposed to be above reason or merely muddles supposed to be below it. Their miracles were more normal than our scientific averages; and the Irish blunder was less illogical than the actual logic of events.

For it seems that we live to-day in a world of witchcraft, in which the orchards wither because they prosper, and the multitude of apples

---

[125] *Credo quia impossibile* is Latin for "I believe because it is impossible."

on the apple-tree of itself turns them into forbidden fruit, and makes
the effort to consume them in every sense fruitless. This is the modern economic paradox, which is called Over-Production, or a glut
in the market, and though at first sight it sounds like the wildest
fantasy, it is well to realise in what sense it is the most solid of facts.
Let it be clearly understood, therefore, that as a description of the
objective social situation at this instant in this industrial society, the
paradox is perfectly true. But it is not really true that the contradiction in terms is true. If we take it, not as a description but as a
definition, if we take it as a matter of abstract argument, then certainly the contradiction is untrue, as every contradiction is untrue.
The truth is that a third element has entered into the matter, which
is not mentioned in this abstract statement of it. That element might
be stated in many ways; perhaps the shortest statement of it is in the
fable of the man who sold razors, and afterwards explained to an
indignant customer, with simple dignity, that he had never said the
razors would shave. When asked if razors were not made to shave,
he replied that they were made to sell. That is A Short History of
Trade and Industry During the Nineteenth and Early Twentieth
Centuries.

God made a world of reason as sure as God made little apples (as
the beautiful proverb goes); and God did not make little apples larger
than large apples. It is not true that a man whose apple-tree is loaded
with apples will suffer from a want of apples; though he may indulge
in a waste of apples. But if he never looks upon apples as things to
eat, but always looks on them as things to sell, he will really get into
another sort of complication; which may end in a sort of contradiction. If, instead of producing as many apples as he wants, he produces as many apples as he imagines the whole world wants, with
the hope of capturing the trade of the whole world—then he will
be either successful or unsuccessful in competing with the man next
door who also wants the whole world's trade to himself. Between
them, they will produce so many apples that apples in the market
will be about as valuable as pebbles on the beach. Thus each of
them will find he has very little money in his pocket, with which to
go and buy fresh pears at the fruiterer's shop. If he had never expected

to get fruit at the fruiterer's shop, but had put up his hand and pulled them off his own tree, his difficulty would never have arisen. It seems simple; but at the root of all apple-trees and apple-growing, it is really as simple as that.

Of course I do not mean that the practice is at present simple; for no practical problem is simple, least of all at the present time, when everything is confused by the corrupt and evasive muddlers who are called practical politicians. But the principle is simple; and the only way to proceed through a complex situation is to start with the right first principle. How far we can do without, or control, or merely modify the disadvantages of buying and selling is quite another matter. But the disadvantages do arise from buying and selling, and not from producing: not even from over-producing. And it is some satisfaction to realise that we are not living in a nightmare in which No is the same as Yes; that even the modern world has not actually gone mad, with all its ingenious attempts to do so; that two and two do in fact make four; and that the man who has four apples really has more than the man who has three. For some modern metaphysicians and moral philosophers seem disposed to leave us in doubt on these points. It is not the fundamental reason in things that is at fault; it is a particular hitch or falsification, arising from a very recent trick of regarding everything only in relation to trade. Trade is all very well in its way, but Trade has been put in the place of Truth. Trade, which is in its nature a secondary or dependent thing, has been treated as a primary and independent thing; as an absolute. The moderns, mad upon mere multiplication, have even made a plural out of what is eternally singular, in the sense of single. They have taken what all ancient philosophers called the Good, and translated it as the Goods.

I believe that certain mystics, in the American business world, protested against the slump by pinning labels to their coats inscribed, "Trade Is Good," along with other similar proclamations, such as, "Capone Is Dead," or "Cancer Is Pleasant," or "Death Is Abolished," or any other hard realistic truths for which they might find space upon their persons. But what interests me about these magicians is that, having decided to call up ideal conditions by means of spells and incantations to control the elements, they did not (so to speak) understand the elements of the elements. They did not go to the root of the matter, and imagine that their troubles had really come to an end. Rather they worshipped the means instead of the end. While they were about it, they ought to have said, not "Trade Is Good," but "Living Is Good," or "Life Is Good." I suppose it would be too much to expect such thoroughly respectable people to say, "God Is Good"; but it is really true that their conception of what is good lacks the philosophical finality that belonged to the goodness of God. When God looked on created things and saw that they were good, it meant that they were good in themselves and as they stood; but by the modern mercantile idea, God would only have looked at them and seen that they were The Goods. In other words, there would be a label tied to the tree or the hill, as to the hat of the Mad Hatter, with "This Style, 10/6." All the flowers and birds would be ticketed with their reduced prices; all the creation would be for sale or all the creatures seeking employment; with all the morning stars making sky-signs together and all the Sons of God shouting for jobs. In other words, these people are incapable of imagining any good except that which comes from bartering something for something else. The idea of a man enjoying a thing in itself, for himself, is inconceivable to them. The notion of a man eating his own apples off his own apple-tree seems like a fairy-tale. Yet the fall from that first creation that was called good has very largely come from the restless impotence for valuing things in themselves; the madness of the trader who cannot see any good in a good, except as something to get rid of. It was once admitted that with sin and death there entered the world something that we call change. It is none the less true and tragic, because what we called change, we called afterwards exchange. Anyhow, the result of that extravagance of exchange has been that when there are too many apples there are too few apple-eaters. I do not insist on the symbol of Eden, or the parable of the apple-tree, but it is odd to notice that even that accidental image pursues us at every stage of this strange story. The last result of treating a tree as a shop or a store instead of as a storeroom, the last effect of treating apples as goods rather than as good, has been in a desperate drive of public charity and in poor men selling apples in the street.

In all normal civilisations the trader existed and must exist. But in all normal civilisations the trader was the exception; certainly he was never the rule; and most certainly he was never the ruler. The predominance which he has gained in the modern world is the cause of all the disasters of the modern world. The universal habit of humanity has been to produce and consume as part of the same process; largely conducted by the same people in the same place. Sometimes goods were produced and consumed on the same great feudal manor; sometimes even on the same small peasant farm. Sometimes there was a tribute from serfs as yet hardly distinguishable from slaves; sometimes there was a co-operation between free-men which the superficial can hardly distinguish from communism. But none of these many historical methods, whatever their vices or limitions, was strangled in the particular tangle of our own time; because most of the people, for most of the time, were thinking about growing food and then eating it; not entirely about growing food and selling it at the stiffest price to somebody who had nothing to eat. And I for one do not believe that there is any way out of the modern tangle, except to increase the proportion of the people who are living according to the ancient simplicity. Nobody in his five wits proposes that there should be no trade and no traders. Nevertheless, it is important to remember, as a matter of mere logic, that there might conceivably be great wealth, even if there were no trade and no traders. It is important for the sort of man whose only hope is that Trade Is Good or whose only secret terror is that Trade Is Bad. In principle, prosperity might be very great, even if trade were very bad. If a village were so fortunately situated that, for some reason, it was easy for every family to keep its own chickens, to grow its own vegetables, to milk its own cow and (I will add) to brew its own beer, the standard of life and property might be very high indeed, even though the long memory of the Oldest Inhabitant only recorded two or three pure transactions of trade; if he could only recall the one far-off event of his neighbour buying a new hat from a gipsy's barrow; or the singular incident of Farmer Billings purchasing an umbrella.

As I have said, I do not imagine, or desire, that things would ever be quite so simple as that. But we must understand things in their simplicity before we can explain or correct their complexity. The complexity of commercial society has become intolerable, because that society is commercial and nothing else. The whole mind of the community is occupied, not with the idea of possessing things, but with the idea of passing them on. When the simple enthusiasts already mentioned say that Trade is Good, they mean that all the people who possess goods are perpetually parting with them. These Optimists presumably invoke the poet, with some slight emendation of the poet's meaning, when he cries aloud, 'Our souls are love and a perpetual farewell.' In that sense, our individualistic and commercial modern society is actually the very reverse of a society founded on Private Property. I mean that the actual direct and isolated enjoyment of private property, as distinct from the excitement of exchanging it or getting a profit on it, is rather rarer than in many simple communities that seem almost communal in their simplicity. In the case of this sort of private consumption, which is also private production, it is very unlikely that it will run continually into overproduction. There is a limit to the number of apples a man can eat, and there will probably be a limit, drawn by his rich and healthy hatred of work, to the number of apples which he will produce but cannot eat. But there is no limit to the number of apples he may possibly sell; and he soon becomes a pushing, dexterous and successful Salesman and turns the whole world upsidedown. For it is he who produces this huge pantomimic paradox with which this rambling reflection began. It is he who makes a wilder revolution than the apple of Adam which was the loosening of death, or the apple of Newton which was the apocalypse of gravitation, by proclaiming the supreme blasphemy and heresy, that the apple was made for the market and not for the mouth. It was he, by starting the wild race of pouring endless apples into a bottomless market, who opened the abyss of irony and contradiction into which we are staring to-day. That trick of treating the trade as the test, and the only test, has left us face to face with a piece of stark staring nonsense written in gigantic letters across the world;

more gigantic than all its own absurd advertisements and announce-ments; the statement that the more we produce the less we possess.

Oscar Wilde would probably have fainted with equal prompti-tude, if told he was being used in an argument about American salesmanship, or in defence of a thrifty and respectable family life on the farm. But it does so happen that one true epigram, among many of his false epigrams, sums up correctly and compactly a certain truth, not (I am happy to say) about Art, but about all that he desired to separate from Art; ethics and even economics. He said in one of his plays: "A cynic is a man who knows the price of everything and the value of nothing." [126] It is extraordinarily true; and the answer to most other things that he said. But it is yet more extraordinary that the modern men who make that mistake most obviously are not the cynics. On the contrary, they are those who call themselves the Optimists; perhaps even those who would call themselves the Idealists; certainly those who regard themselves as the Regular Guys and the Sons of Service and Uplift. It is too often those very people who have spoilt all their good effect, and weakened their considerable good example in work and social con-tact, by that very error: that things are to be judged by the price and not by the value. And since Price is a crazy and incalculable thing, while Value is an intrinsic and indestructible thing, they have swept us into a society which is no longer solid but fluid, as unfath-omable as a sea and as treacherous as a quicksand. Whether any-thing more solid can be built again upon a social philosophy of values, there is now no space to discuss at length here; but I am certain that nothing solid can be built on any other philosophy; certainly not upon the utterly unphilosophical philosophy of blind buying and selling; of bullying people into purchasing what they do not want; of making it badly so that they may break it and imagine they want it again; of keeping rubbish in rapid circulation like a dust-storm in a desert; and pretending that you are teaching men to hope, because you do not leave them one intelligent instant in which to despair.

[126] The quotation is from *Lady Windermere's Fan* (1892).

SEX AND PROPERTY

In the dull, dusty, stale, stiff-jointed and lumbering language, to which most modern discussion is limited, it is necessary to say that there is at this moment the same fashionable fallacy about Sex and about Property. In the older and freer language, in which men could both speak and sing, it is truer to say that the same evil spirit has blasted the two great powers that make the poetry of life; the Love of Woman and the Love of the Land. It is important to observe, to start with, that the two things were closely connected so long as humanity was human, even when it was heathen. Nay, they were still closely connected, even when it was a decadent heathenism. But even the stink of decaying heathenism has not been so bad as the stink of decaying Christianity. The corruption of the best....

For instance, there were throughout antiquity, both in its first stage and its last, modes of idolatry and imagery of which Christian men can hardly speak. "Let them not be so much as named among you." [127] Men wallowed in the mere sexuality of a mythology of sex; they organised prostitution like priesthood, for the service of their temples; they made pornography their only poetry; they paraded emblems that turned even architecture into a sort of cold and colossal exhibitionism. Many learned books have been written of all these phallic cults; and anybody can go to them for the details, for all I care. But what interests me is this:

In one way all this ancient sin was infinitely superior, immeasurably superior, to the modern sin. All those who write of it at least agree on one fact; that it was the cult of Fruitfulness. It was unfortunately too often interwoven, very closely, with the cult of the fruitfulness of the land. It was at least on the side of Nature. It was at least on the side of Life. It has been left to the last Christians, or rather to the first Christians fully committed to blaspheming and denying Christianity, to invent a new kind of worship of Sex, which is not even a worship of Life. It has been left to the

---

[127] The quotation is from Ephesians 5:3.

very latest Modernists to proclaim an erotic religion which at once
exalts lust and forbids fertility. The new Paganism literally merits
the reproach of Swinburne, when mourning for the old Paganism:
"and rears not the bountiful token and spreads not the fatherly
feast." The new priests abolish the fatherhood and keep the feast—to
themselves. They are worse than Swinburne's Pagans. The priests
of Priapus and Cotytto[128] go into the kingdom of heaven before
them.

   Now it is not unnatural that this unnatural separation, between
sex and fruitfulness, which even the Pagans would have thought a
perversion, has been accompanied with a similar separation and
perversion about the nature of the love of the land. In both depart-
ments there is precisely the same fallacy; which it is quite possible
to state precisely. The reason why our contemporary countrymen
do not understand what we mean by Property is that they only
think of it in the sense of Money; in the sense of salary; in the
sense of something which is immediately consumed, enjoyed and
expended; something which gives momentary pleasure and disap-
pears. They do not understand that we mean by Property something that includes that pleasure incidentally; but begins and ends
with something far more grand and worthy and creative. The man
who makes an orchard where there has been a field, who owns
the orchard and decides to whom it shall descend, does also enjoy
the taste of apples; and let us hope, also, the taste of cider. But he
is doing something very much grander, and ultimately more grat-
ifying, than merely eating an apple. He is imposing his will upon
the world in the manner of the charter given him by the will of
God; he is asserting that his soul is his own, and does not belong
to the Orchard Survey Department, or the chief Trust in the Apple
Trade. But he is also doing something which was implicit in all
the most ancient religions of the earth; in those great panoramas
of pageantry and ritual that followed the order of the seasons in
China or Babylonia; he is worshipping the fruitfulness of the world.
Now the notion of narrowing property merely to *enjoying* money

---

[128] Priapus and Cotytto are fertility deities.

is exactly like the notion of narrowing love merely to *enjoying* sex. In both cases an incidental, isolated, servile and even secretive pleasure is substituted for participation in a great creative process; even in the everlasting Creation of the world.

The two sinister things can be seen side by side in the system of Bolshevist Russia; for Communism is the only complete and logical working model of Capitalism. The sins are there a system which are everywhere else a sort of repeated blunder. From the first, it is admitted, that the whole system was directed towards encouraging or driving the worker to spend his wages; to have nothing left on the next pay day; to enjoy everything and consume everything and efface everything; in short, to shudder at the thought of only one crime; the creative crime of thrift. It was a tame extravagance; a sort of disciplined dissipation; a meek and submissive prodigality. For the moment the slave left off drinking all his wages, the moment he began to hoard or hide any property, he would be saving up something which might ultimately purchase his liberty. He might begin to count for something in the State; that is, he might become less of a slave and more of a citizen. Morally considered, there has been nothing quite so unspeakably mean as this Bolshevist generosity. But it will be noted that exactly the same spirit and tone pervades the manner of dealing with the other matter. Sex also is to come to the slave merely as a pleasure; that it may never be a power. He is to know as little as possible, or at least to think as little as possible, of the pleasure as anything else except a pleasure; to think or know nothing of where it comes from or where it will go to, when once the soiled object has passed through his own hands. He is not to trouble about its origin in the purposes of God or its sequel in the posterity of man. In every department he is not a possessor, but only a consumer; even if it be of the first elements of life and fire in so far as they are consumable; he is to have no notion of the sort of Burning Bush that burns and is not consumed. For that bush only grows on the soil, on the real land where human beings can behold it; and the spot on which they stand is holy ground. Thus there is an exact parallel between the two modern moral, or immoral, ideas of social reform. The world has forgotten simultaneously that the making of a Farm is something much larger than the making of a profit, or even a product, in the sense of liking the taste of beetroot sugar; and that the founding of a Family is something much larger than sex in the limited sense of current literature; which was anticipated in one bleak and blinding flash in a single line of George Meredith; "And eat our pot of honey on the grave." [129]

---

[129] The Meredith quotation is from *Modern Love* (1862).

ST. THOMAS MORE

Most would understand the phrase that the mind of More was like a diamond that a tyrant threw away into a ditch, because he could not break it. It is but a metaphor; but it does sometimes happen that the metaphor is many-sided, like the diamond. What moved the tyrant to a sort of terror of that mind was its clarity; it was the very reverse of a cloudy crystal filled only with opalescent dreams or visions of the past. The King and his great Chancellor had been companions as well as contemporaries; in many ways, both were Renaissance men; but in some ways, the man who was the more Catholic was the less medieval. That is, there was perhaps more in the Tudor of that mere musty fag-end of decayed medievalism, which the real Renaissance reformers felt to be the corruption of the time. In More's mind there was nothing but clarity; in Henry's mind, though he was no fool and certainly no Protestant, there was something of confused conservatism. Like many a better man who is an Anglo-Catholic, he had a touch of the antiquary. Thomas More was a better rationalist, which was why there was nothing in his religion that was merely local, or in that sense merely loyal. More's mind was like a diamond also in a power like that of cutting glass; of cutting through things that seemed equally transparent, but were at once less solid and less many-sided. For the true consistent heresies generally look very clear indeed; like Calvinism then or Communism now. They sometimes even look very true; they sometimes even are very true, in the limited sense of a truth that is less than the Truth. They are at once more thin and more brittle than the diamond. For a heresy is not often a mere lie; as Thomas More himself said, "Never was there a heretic that spoke all false." A heresy is a truth that hides all the other truths. A mind like More's was full of light like a house made of windows; but the windows looked out on all sides and in all directions. We might say that, as the jewel has many facets, so the man had many faces; only none of them were masks.

Thus there are so many aspects of this great story, that the difficulty of dealing with it in an article is one of selection, and even

175

more of proportion. I might attempt and fail to do justice to its highest aspect; to that holiness which now stands beyond even Beatitude;[130] I might equally fill the whole space with the homeliest of the jokes in which the great humorist delighted in daily life; perhaps the biggest joke of all being the book called Utopia. The nineteenth century Utopians imitated the book without seeing the joke. But among a bewildering complexity of such different aspects or angles, I have decided to deal only with two points; not because they were the most important truths about Thomas More, though their importance is very great; but because they are two of the most important truths about the world at this present moment. One appears most clearly in his death and the other in his life; one, perhaps we should rather say, concerns his public life and the other his private life; one is far beyond any adequate admiration and the other may seem in comparison an almost comic bathos; but one hits exactly the right nail on the head in our present discussion about the State; and the other about the Family.

Thomas More died the death of a traitor for defying absolute monarchy; in the strict sense of treating monarchy as an absolute. He was willing, and even eager, to respect it as a relative thing, but not as an absolute thing. The heresy that had just raised its head in his own time was the heresy called the Divine Right of Kings. In that form it is now regarded as an old superstition; but it has already reappeared as a very new superstition, in the form of the Divine Right of Dictators. But most people still vaguely think of it as old; and nearly all of them think it is much older than it is. One of the chief difficulties to-day is to explain to people that this idea was not native to medieval or many older times. People know that the constitutional checks on kings have been increasing for a century or two; they do not realize that any other kind of checks could ever have operated; and in the changed conditions those other checks are hard to describe or imagine. But most certainly medieval men thought of the king as ruling *sub deo et lege*; rightly translated, "under God and the law," but also involving something atmospheric that might

---

[130] Chesterton is referring to More, who was canonized in 1935.

more vaguely be called, "under the morality implied in all our institutions." Kings were excommunicated, were deposed, were assassinated, were dealt with in all sorts of defensible and indefensible ways; but nobody thought the whole commonwealth fell with the king, or that he alone had ultimate authority there. The State did not own men so entirely, even when it could send them to the stake, as it sometimes does now where it can send them to the elementary school. There was an idea of refuge, which was generally an idea of sanctuary. In short, in a hundred strange and subtle ways, as we should think them, there was a sort of escape upwards. There were limits to Caesar; and there was liberty with God.

The highest voice of the Church has pronounced that this hero was in the true and traditional sense a Saint and Martyr. And it is appropriate to remember that he does indeed stand, for a rather special reason, with those first Martyrs whose blood was the seed of the Church in the very earliest pagan persecutions. For most of them died, as he did, for refusing to extend a civil loyalty into a religious idolatry. Most of them did not die for refusing to worship Mercury or Venus, or fabulous figures who might be supposed not to exist; or others like Moloch or Priapus whom we might well hope do not exist. Most of them died for refusing to worship somebody who certainly did exist; and even somebody whom they were quite prepared to obey but not to worship. The typical martyrdom generally turned on the business of burning incense before the statue of Divus Augustus; the sacred image of the Emperor. He was not necessarily a demon to be destroyed; he was simply a despot who must not be turned into a deity. That is where their case came so very close to the practical problem of Thomas More; and so very near to the practical problem of mere State-worship to-day. And it is typical of all Catholic thought that men died in torments, not because their foes "spoke all false"; but simply because they would not give an unreasonable reverence where they were perfectly prepared to give a reasonable respect. For us the problem of Progress is always a problem of Proportion; improvement is reaching a right proportion; not merely moving in one direction. And our doubts about most modern developments, about the Socialists in the last generation, or the

Fascists in this generation, do not arise from our having any doubts at all about the desirability of economic justice, or of national order, any more than Thomas More bothered his head to object to a hereditary monarchy. He objected to the Divine Right of Kings.

In the very deepest sense he is thus the champion of Liberty in his public life and his still more public death. In his private life he is the type of a truth even less understood to-day; the truth that the real habitation of Liberty is the home. Modern novels and newspapers and problem plays have been piled up in one huge rubbish-heap to hide this simple fact; yet it is a fact that can be proved quite simply. Public life must be rather more regimented than private life; just as a man cannot wander about in the traffic of Piccadilly exactly as he could wander about in his own garden. Where there is traffic there will be regulation of traffic; and this is quite as true, or even more true, where it is what we should call an illicit traffic; where the most modern governments organize sterilization to-day and may organize infanticide to-morrow. Those who hold the modern superstition that the State can do no wrong will be bound to accept such a thing as right. If individuals have any hope of protecting their freedom, they must protect their family life. At the worst there will be rather more personal adaptation in a household than in a concentration camp; at the best there will be rather less routine in a family than in a factory. In any tolerably healthy home the rules are at least partly affected by things that cannot possibly affect fixed laws; for instance, the thing we call a sense of humour.

Therefore More is vividly important as the Humorist; as representing that special phase of the Humanist. Behind his public life, which was so grand a tragedy, there was a private life that was a perpetual comedy. He was, as Mr. Christopher Hollis says in his excellent study, "an incorrigible leg-puller." Everybody knows, of course, that the comedy and the tragedy met as they meet in Shakespeare, on that last high wooden stage where his drama ended. In that terrible moment he realized and relished the grand joke of the human body, as of a sort of lovable lumber; gravely discussed whether his beard had committed treason; and said in hoisting himself up the ladder, "See me safely up; coming down I can take care of myself."

But Thomas More never came down that ladder. He had done with all descents and downward goings, and what had been himself vanished from men's eyes almost in the manner of his Master, who being lifted up shall draw all men after Him. And the dark closed over him and the clouds came between; until long afterwards the wisdom that can read such secrets saw him fixed far above our heads like a returning star; and established his station in the skies.

THE RETURN OF CÆSAR

Whether or no it be an example of first and second childhood, I sometimes have a whimsical fancy that I shall end as I began, trying to make some sense out of what is called Liberalism in politics. There is a Fleet Street story about me, which may be a fact though I have entirely forgotten it, that when I was asked if I was a Liberal, I answered, "I am the only Liberal." It will be agreed that, in these days, I should be very nearly the only Liberal. But I hope nobody will accuse me of wanting to be a Liberal leader. The Liberal Party now consists entirely of leaders—or rather misleaders. And all they want, all they have left to pray for, is one single simple solitary human being who is willing to be misled. On second thoughts, I rather doubt whether I will offer myself even to fulfil this humble office; whatever may be my qualifications for filling all the seats at a public meeting, and constituting the whole audience, while my five leaders address me from the platform, urging me to five urgent but incompatible courses of action. No, the sense in which I have again become conscious of the existence of purely political Liberalism is not so much due to what remains of it, as to what has vanished from it; not to what the Liberals say as to what they do not say. In the face of fashionable Fascism, and the toppling simplifications of the Totalitarian State, there really is a great deal that ought to be said for Liberalism; or, in clearer language, for Liberty.

Many things return; and thank God we live now in a time when we can talk once more about Church and State; though nowadays it generally means the Catholic Church and the Totalitarian State. But at least we have abolished the most illiberal of the illiberal limitations of Liberalism. We can recognise religion in history at the back of European ideas, including modern ideas; and in this connection the story of Church and State is very strange indeed. Of course, the one thing that has really confused the story of Church and State is the thing called the State Church. But that is a mere illogical interlude; in which God holds his authority from Caesar; instead of Caesar holding it from God. The normal relation between Church and State, through most of the varied phases of history, has not been exactly an establishment, but something more like what we have seen reappear in Germany. When there was not a conflict, there was a Concordat. It will be noted that the Church generally had a Concordat with her enemies rather than her friends. There was a dispute with Napoleon and a Concordat with Napoleon: a dispute with Mussolini and a Concordat with Mussolini; a dispute with Hitler and a Concordat with Hitler. And though the word would not perhaps have been used, and would not perhaps have been correct, something of the same paradox broods like a suspended storm over the State and Church in their relations in even earlier times. It marks the Church in her relation with the Roman Emperors; in her relation with the Greek Emperors; in her relation with the German Emperors. There was always some sort of Concordat, and there was never any complete concord.

It needs nearly a lifetime to trace the curve or orbit of the Church, and the rhythm of things returning. But to one growing up as a Liberal, and in many ways still a Liberal, the chief interest of the last days is in this. The Church, roughly speaking, almost always remains at about the same distance from the State and its experiments. There are exceptions, of course; when an Emperor persecutes the Church or the Church excommunicates an Emperor. The Church could hardly be expected to concord very much, even in the coldest manner, with Nero or the No-God Movement in Moscow. But it is most often found at about the same distance from the State as it is now from the Totalitarian State. Leo XIII stood at about that distance from the French Republican State. Few Catholics need originally have stood at any much greater distance even from the French Revolution. But the very names will serve to remind us of the vital point at issue. It is the State that changes; it is the State that destroys; it is nearly always the State that persecutes. The Totalitarian State is now making a clean sweep of *all* our old notions of liberty, even more than the French Revolution made a clean sweep of all the old ideas of loyalty. It is the Church that excommunicates; but, in that very word, implies that a communion stands open for a restored communicant. It is the State that *exterminates*; it is the State that abolishes absolutely and altogether; whether it is the American State abolishing beer, or the Fascist State abolishing parties, or the Hitlerite State abolishing almost everything but itself.

Now suppose, for the sake of argument, that I did become again merely an ordinary Liberal, as the term was understood when I was active in Liberal politics. Suppose I thought the time had come to remind men that there really is an intellectual advantage in hearing all sides; a help to order in a measure of liberty; a healthy irritation in government by debate. Suppose I said (as I do say) that every government ought to be checked by an opposition; suppose I said (as I do not say) that free international exchange is demonstrably better than all this economic nationalism. Suppose I said that recognised majority rule is better than random minority rule; suppose I said that Democracy as a failure is better than Dictatorship as a success. I could say all this, and much more, and remain a quite ordinary and orthodox member of the ancient Church. But I could not say it, over a great part of the modern world, without being punished by the modern State. Rome with its religious authority would not silence me. But Fascism with its secular authority would silence me. Bolshevism with its secular authority would silence me. Hitlerism with its secular authority would silence me. When I began to live and (alas) to write, all the other Liberals had inherited a huge legend that all persecution had come from the Church. Some of them still mumble old memories about the Spanish Inquisition (a thing started strictly by the State); with the fact staring them in the face that the actual persecution now going on in Spain is the spoliation of Spaniards, simply because they are Catholic priests and schoolmasters. But anyhow, it was supposed that what was called superstition was somehow the mother of persecution. I appeal to all my fellow-Liberals to admit that the facts have flatly contradicted this idea. Every Catholic enjoys much more freedom in Catholicism than any Liberal does under Bolshevism or Fascism. I might have been a Liberal and belonged to the Centrum[131] in Germany or the

---

[131] The Centrum refers to the Center Party, a Catholic political party established in Germany in 1871.

Partito Popolare in Italy; it is not the Church but the State that would stop me. For the State has returned with all its ancient terrors out of antiquity; with the Gods of the City thundering from the sky and, marching with the pageant in iron panoply the ghosts of a hundred tyrants; and we have begun to understand in what wide fields and playgrounds of liberty, the Faith that made us free has so long allowed us to wander and to play.

AUSTRIA

Last year, the representative of all that remains of the Holy Roman Empire was murdered by the barbarians. As an atrocity it has been adequately denounced; and it breeds in some of us rather a dumb sort of disgust, almost as if it had been done not by barbarians but by beasts. Perhaps the only further fact to be noted, on that side, is the fact that this is the only kind of effort in which these clumsy people are not merely clumsy. The Nordic man of the Nazi type in Germany is a very slow thinker, and incredibly backward and behind the times in science and philosophy. That is why, for instance, he clings to the word "Aryan," as if he were his own great-grandfather laboriously poring over the first pages of Max Muller,[132] under the concentrated stare of the astounded ethnologists of later days. He is slow in a great many things; as, for instance, in releasing prisoners who are admittedly innocent; or in answering questions put by foreign critics or Catholic bishops. We have good reason to know that he is slow in paying his debts; to the point of ceasing to pay them. He is very slow in bringing about the Utopia that he promised to the German people; the complete financial stability and the total disappearance of unemployment. He is slow in a thousand things, from the length of his meals to the lengthiness of his metaphysics. But in one thing he is not slow but almost slick. He is swift to shed innocent blood; he really has a certain technique in the matter of murdering other people; and the prospect of this sport alone can move him to an animation that is almost human. Hitler really killed quite a creditable number of people for one week-end holiday; and the assassination of Dollfuss did show some touch of that efficiency, which the Nazis once promised to display in other fields of activity.

But it is much more important to insist on the large human and historic matters mentioned at the beginning of this article. Dollfuss died like a loyal and courageous man, asking forgiveness for his

[132] Friedrich Max Müller (1823–1900) was a German-born Oxford professor and authority on philology, mythology and comparative religions.

murderers; and the souls of the just are in the hands of God, how-ever much their enemies (with that mark of mere mud that is stamped over all they do) take a pleasure in denying them the help of their religion. But Dollfuss dead, even more than Dollfuss living, is also a symbol of something of immense moment to mankind, which is practically never mentioned by our politicians or our papers. We call it for convenience Austria; in a sense we might more truly call it Europe; but, above all (for this is the vital and quite neglected fact), it would be strictly correct and consistent with history to call it Germany. The very fact that the name of "Germany" has been taken from the Austrians and given to the Prussians sums up the tragedy of three hundred years. It was the tale of the war waged by the barbarians against the Empire; the real original German Empire. It began with the first Prussian shot in the Thirty Years' War; it ended with the shot that killed the Austrian Chancellor.

Whether we call it the Empire, or the Old Germany, or the cul-ture of the Danube, what Austria meant and means is this. That it is normal for Europeans, even for Germans, to be civilised; that it is normal for Europeans, even for Germans, to be Christians; and, we must in historic honesty add, normal for them to be Catholics. This culture always incurred the hatred of the barbarians to the north-east; and in the nineteenth century a barbarian of genius, named Bismarck, actually managed to transfer to Prussia the prestige that had always normally belonged to Austria. That is the broad fact which is always left out in all modern enlightened discussion; for it involves two things; an elementary knowledge of history, which is rare, and an elementary knowledge of recent history, which is much rarer than a knowledge of ancient history. There is always a chance that about six politicians have heard of the Roman Empire; and perhaps two and a half politicians have even heard of the Holy Roman Empire. Among the scholarly leader-writers who have hitherto hardly noticed the existence of the Austrians, there are some who have read some-thing about the Ostro-Goths[133] or perhaps (if they are very scholarly)

[133] Ostro-Goths were the eastern division of the Goths, who invaded Italy in the late fifth century.

really do know much more about Austrasians[134] than about Austrians. It is sometimes possible to arouse faint interest in anything remotely historic; and always possible to arouse a fashionable fuss about anything prehistoric. But the facts which led up to the facts which stare us in the face, those are known practically to nobody in the age of newspapers. And perhaps next to nobody among our rulers will know what is meant by saying that the filthy butchery at Vienna was but the continuation of a policy, expressed in the invasion of Silesia and the victory of Sadowa.[135]

We have at least learned one lesson to-day; that old things return. This is simply that very old remembrance of our race; the barbarian invasion. This is not the Corporative State; or the Fascist Theory; or the thousand theories, including our own, for improving our ancient civilisation. This is the Turks besieging Vienna. If indeed it be not an injustice to the stately, the stable and the reverent religion of Mahomet to compare it with the feverish fads and fallacies that chase each other across the half-baked and half-baptized Teutonism of the North. This is, at least, what all men meant by the Turks besieging Vienna. It is the centre of our civilisation in peril; it is the blow of the barbarian when for once, in his blindness, he happens to aim at the heart.

---

[134] Austriasians were the eastern division of the kingdom of the Franks.

[135] Chesterton is referring to the invasion of Austrian Silesia in 1740 by the Prussian armies of Frederick II. The victory of Sadowa was the Prussian defeat of Austria in 1866.

THE SCRIPTURE READER

Mr. Bernard Shaw has written a very Protestant tract,[136] on the paramount duty of reading the Bible, and especially of re-reading the Bible; of course in the light of Private Judgment. For Private Judgment is never wrong, just as Private Property is never right. It is something of a triumph to have carried principles so entangled and contradictory, unchanged, untroubled and unenlightened, through a long and valuable life. Some technical difficulties may still prevent Mr. Shaw's Bible tract from being included in the literature of the British and Foreign Bible Society; but I should imagine that they would soon be overcome; now that the old stuff that calls itself the Modern Mind has become such a muddy amalgam of Puritanism and Modernism that it does not matter, so long as a man reads his Bible, whether he denies his God. But I, who love and admire Bernard Shaw, cannot help being sorry that he should have returned from the land of the Boers so completely transformed into a Baptist missionary beginning to have doubts about Habakkuk. Perhaps it is a judgment on him for having supported the Imperialists in the Boer War; because the Webbs had the truly wonderful notion that it was "practical."

Of course, like every other sectarian "Scripture-reader," Mr. Shaw re-reads the Bible and finds something different from what the last sectarian found. That is the whole fun and futility of this "Sunday game," which has now been played for nearly four hundred years, and is about played out. But the old sectaries, who discovered Calvinism or Quakerism or Mormonism in the Bible, at least had the tenacity to keep hold of what they found; and finish their programme logically. But, alas, Mr. Shaw is a true Modernist in the fact that he cannot complete even his own argument, for fear it should end by proving something. His new theory of Holy Scripture is broadly this; that the Old Testament Prophets were each of them dealing with a different God; though they seem to have been under

[136] Chesterton is referring to the *Adventures of a Black Girl in Search of God* (1932).

the impression that it was the same God. Thus the God of Job is better than the God of Noah; the God of Micah is better than the God of Job and therefore ... therefore what? The obvious logical conclusion of the argument would be that the God-Man of the Christians, the Second Person of the Trinity, was better than the God of Micah; and rightly replaced him on progressive principles. But here, of course, Mr. Shaw goes all to pieces; wildly reverses the whole of his own theory of theistic improvement, and collapses, muttering some nonsense about the psychological misfortunes of Jesus. That is only one part of the book; but it is typical of the whole of this jointless inconsequent modern way of writing. Pages upon pages are devoted to showing that primitive gods were leading up to something greater and more splendid; and it is perfectly obvious what they did actually lead up to. But the moment the Modernist sees it, he runs away from it.

The actual story of the Black Girl seems to be modelled on *Candide*; indeed much of it takes place in the famous garden of Voltaire. It was not really a very wide garden; indeed, it was a narrow garden, but it was a neat garden, according to the Dutch gardening of the period: and it is almost a relief after the jungle of journalese that is now called modern thought. Voltaire, unlike Shaw, had a straightforward and logical plan for his story. Candide is a youth brought up by a German professor in a very nonsensical philosophy called Optimism; like many nonsensical philosophies taught by German professors. It was to the effect that everything in this world fits in with our peace and comfort; whatever else it was, it was almost the opposite of Catholicism, or even Protestantism; for Christians had, if anything, rather exaggerated the truth that life is a vale of tears and a place of trial; that peace could only be found in the monastery or justice on the Day of Judgment. But Voltaire has no difficulty in showing how real life knocked this Teutonic heresy of Optimism to pieces. But it marks the more muddled modern mentality that we do not really know, at the end of Mr. Shaw's parable, what it is that has been knocked to pieces; or whether the Black Girl has found God, or failed to find God, or found that there is no God to find. Anyhow, she has found Mr. Bernard Shaw, who is acting as Voltaire's gardener, but has not yet learnt the lucid style and thought of his employer. It must be a comfort to Mr. Shaw at least to know that he is truly a Proletarian. Voltaire said that a man should cultivate his garden. It is the measure of Progress that he has since apparently become a servant cultivating his master's garden.

For the rest, I know there are many simple people who will console and gratify my old friend by being duly shocked at various passages in his book. It would be almost cruel to deprive him of such comfort; but I confess that I myself remained cold, and could not get anything resembling a decent shock out of the whole business. It always seems to me that we must face the question of whether we are dealing with believers or unbelievers; and only a believer can be a blasphemer. We Catholics must realise that by this time we are living in pagan lands; and that the barbarians around us know not what they do. Of course, those who think Jesus was an ordinary man will talk of Him in an ordinary way. What I complain of is that, even then, they cannot talk of Him in a sensible way. For instance, Mr. Shaw has a long dialogue in which his imaginary Jesus feebly implies the idea that everything can be solved by love, and apparently love of any kind. Now there is not a grain of evidence that the historical Jesus of Nazareth ever said that any such emotion, selfish or sensual or sentimental, must be a substitute for everything else everywhere. Rousseau and the Romantics, in the time of Voltaire, sometimes said something a little like it; and the Church resisted it from the beginning, just as Bernard Shaw wakes up to resist it in the end. It is much more important for us to point out that the attack on the Faith breaks down, by its own folly on its own ground, than to express our own feelings about some of the random results of its invincible ignorance, when it stumbles upon ground more sacred.

AN EXPLANATION

The last two essays in this collection have so obviously the character of newspaper correspondence, that a word must be added about the circumstances of their appearance. At the request of the B.B.C., I gave an address in their series on Freedom about the Catholic view of the matter; an address which was very much criticised; but I sometimes fancy that the most deadly criticism was involuntary and unconscious. For I could not help feeling that some of my critics must have gone to sleep, and snatched a brief respite from the recital, only to wake again with a start and all the bewilderments of nightmare, to hear the ruthless infliction still going on. I should be the last to blame them; I sometimes nearly go to sleep myself when listening to myself, let alone to anybody so remote from me as I must naturally be from them. But the actual effect, anyhow, was that most of the agonised questions which they asked me afterwards I had already answered before they were asked. At the beginning of the whole address, I explained the beginning of the whole business; that I had been specially asked to speak as a Catholic and therefore as a controversialist. If they asked Sir Oswald Mosley[137] to explain why he was a Fascist, it might or might not be popular; but it would be a little hard on Sir Oswald to complain that he had dragged the subject of Fascism into politics, or the subject of politics into the B.B.C. Yet to read some of the innocent criticism I have read, one would really suppose I had been asked to give a literary lecture on Milton or Shelley, and had seized the opportunity to deliver a wild eulogy upon Torquemada and Guy Fawkes. If indeed, in this free country where (I am assured) all views can be expressed, it is unpardonable to suggest that the Protestant view of Freedom is wrong, some responsibility must be shared by those who ask the Catholic to explain why the Catholic view is right. For that peculiar diplomatic and tactful art of saying that Catholicism is true, without suggesting

[137] Oswald Mosley (1896–1980) was the founder of the British Union of Fascists in 1932.

for one moment that anti-Catholicism is false, is an art which I am too old a Rationalist to learn at my time of life.

The second legend that arose out of hearing, or not hearing, my wireless speech, was an extraordinary delusion that I made a speech about drink. Out of nineteen hundred words, the newspapers seemed to have selected three words, in the form of the polished epigram, "I like beer." Now I fear I am so constituted by cultural tradition, that I cannot for the life of me see anything more comic, or eccentric, or provocative, or sensational, about saying, "I like beer," than about saying, "I like bananas." But I do most certainly see that there would be something both egotistical and trivial about saying, "I like bananas," if it were not a part of an ordinary objective argument. And my remark was a part of an objective argument. Only I was arguing for the exact opposite of what they imagine. I said it was well to remember, to start with, that an ordinary poor man from Catholic countries would find what he regarded as ancient universal popular liberties forbidden in Protestant countries. The obvious instances are Prohibition and the veto on the Irish Sweepstake. I then said that these lighter instances were balanced indifferently for me, because "I like beer; there is nothing that bores me quite so much as horse-racing. But I have some sense of human rights." In short, it is self-evident that I only said I like beer in order to show that it did not matter a curse what I liked. Yet in face of this fact, an excellent cultivated weekly paper declared that I should not like Liberty if I did not like beer. The editor handsomely admitted the fact when I drew his attention to it, and my quarrel is not here with him. But further comments were made in the matter, which are the text of one of these two essays.

For the rest, if any one doubts that there is such a thing as Catholic liberty, I think it can do no harm to let him realise that there is such a thing as Catholic controversy; I mean controversy between Catholics. I have, therefore, included here my reply to some frank and friendly but very definite doubts about my action, that were expressed in one of the very best of the modern Catholic papers. For I feel it would not be fair to answer somewhat controversially a criticism in an Anglican organ, while in any way concealing the fact that I have been criticised also in an organ of my own communion. It will also be clear from the context, I think, that a distinguished Italian, Dr. Crespi, who speaks specially as an opponent of Fascism, attacked me at a slightly different angle. And this alone would illustrate the main fact; that the substance of my speech was concerned with all sorts of large modern problems, and had no more to do with my taste in beer than with my familiar appearance as a fashionable figure at Ascot. I pointed out that, by limiting liberty to preaching and printing, we had given a huge advantage to cranks over common Christian people; that we had lost a peasantry and were living under a plutocracy. Indeed, some critics combined the contradictory accusations; having proved that I was wholly concentrated upon booze and betting, they rushed on to rend the sky with cries against my sweeping slanders on the Press, the Parliament, the Landlord System and the British Empire. If they will try compressing all these topics into twenty minutes, they will understand how easy it is for the hearer (even if he manages to keep awake) to miss the proportion and the point.

WHY PROTESTANTS PROHIBIT

It is with mingled respect and regret that I differ from a paper I admire so much as I do the *Catholic Herald*, or a critic for whom I have so much sympathy as I have for Dr. Crespi. I have already said that the *Herald* is nearly the best, or the only newspaper we have; and my confidence in Dr. Crespi's sincerity is so complete that I unhesitatingly accept his assurance that he has both read and heard my address on Liberty; for without that assurance, I might be tempted now and then to think he had done neither. But this distressing exhibition of mine seems to have been such a shock to him as to leave him with a strange impression that I uttered some sort of eulogy, or at least apology, touching Italian Fascism, or more generally, the new dictatorships in Europe. Now as a fact, I was very careful to explain that I did nothing of the sort. I said of such a system that I detested some forms of it, that I did not defend any form of it; that it practically proclaimed itself a tyranny, and that I was quite ready to treat it as a tyranny. What I said was that this tyranny, even if it was a tyranny, had not in fact torn up certain traditions of popular freedom in Catholic countries, which have been, and are being, more and more ruthlessly and rapidly torn up and uprooted in Protestant countries. If I say, "Even Nero never forbade people to grow corn," I am not uttering a eulogy on Nero; and that is the sort of thing I might say about the Prohibitionists who forbade men to drink wine. But there is indeed a curious irony about my two friendly critics on this occasion. My own friendly feeling for the *Herald* is largely founded on the fact that it does print solid blocks of information about what wicked foreigners have to say for themselves, including Fascists and Hitlerites; so that we can judge for ourselves how wicked the foreigners are. And my unfriendly criticism of British plutocracy is largely founded on the fact that its monopolist newspapers never do this; being owned by one or two millionaires ignorant of Europe and interested only in some silly stunt or slogan. In short, I only say that

A letter to the *Catholic Herald*.

if dictators suppress newspapers, newspaper proprietors suppress news. And yet I am rebuked for disliking this, even by those who avoid it.

Similarly, I warmly respect Dr. Crespi for trying to free his country from what he regards as oppression and wrong. But apparently he will not allow me to do the same thing for my country. I fear, on this point, I must be firm with him. I respectfully refuse to allow my native land to be ruined by blindness and pride and hypocrisy, and its heart eaten out by corruption and the worship of wealth; merely in order that Dr. Crespi may have a wholly imaginary England to flourish in the face of Signor Mussolini.

I need not in this space destroy the delusion in detail; because for most English economists (especially Catholics) it is already destroyed. I will only say that his paean in praise of nineteenth-century capitalism would have been very welcome to the rich in the nineteenth century; and greatly encouraged those who laid on the millions a yoke little better than slavery. But I will give him a tip: from one who knows (I make bold to say) more about England than he does. *Whenever he sees our newspapers announcing revival of trade it simply means that employers have found out how to cut down the wage bill.* All recent industrial history here has been a scheme to lower wages; beginning with the triumph of the lock-out that crushed the miners, followed by vindictive laws against Labour after the general strike, and ending by taking advantage of the default on gold, to pay every workman a pound that is not a pound. That is how we do it here. I did not argue whether it is worse when done by a despot or by this anonymous conspiracy. But the tragedy (and to me despotism instead of democracy, even theoretical democracy, is a tragedy) is largely due to reaction against commercial conspiracies. For the rest, let not your Wireless Expert weep for me; or imagine that all will be bewildered who "have not the key." I happen to have stacks of letters from very poor people thanking me for pointing out how the small men are now crushed in England if they attempt independence. They are turned out of house and shop by the hundred, by modern monopolist aggression. They have the key all right; it is called in slang the key of the street. None of them has heard of the Keys of Peter; but, being poor like St. Peter, they know how poor men are goaded in the House of the Governor; and what rage rises in them against the servant of Caiaphas. They support me sufficiently, thank you, in not encouraging the Englishman to play the Pharisee.

The fact is that Protestant tyranny is totally different from Catholic tyranny; let alone Catholic liberty. It is ineradicably rooted in a totally opposite motive and moral philosophy. You seem to suggest that, where Protestant restrictions are really excessive, it is but a part of the normal temptation of officials to magnify their office.

Under your favour, it is nothing of the sort. That is just the point of the whole business. Protestantism is in its nature prone to what may be called Prohibitionism. I do not mean prohibition of drink (though it happens to be a convenient comparison: that none of the ten thousand tyrants of Mediterranean history would ever have dreamed of uprooting the vine, since Pentheus[138] was torn in pieces); I mean that the Protestant tends to prohibit, rather than to curtail or control. His theory of Prohibition is rooted in his theory of progress; which began with expectation of the Millennium; but has ended in similar expectations of the Superman. I have no notion what Dr. Crespi means by my golden age: after Eden I know of no golden age in the past. But Protestant progress does imply a golden age in the future—and one *utterly* cut off or altered from the past. By now this Dawnism is deeply affected by Darwinism. Man is a monkey who has lost his tail and does not want it back. It is not a question of docking his tail, because it takes up too much room; or telling him to curl up his tail and only wave it on festive occasions; as in the Catholic view of discipline and recreation. No men need tails; so they need amputation.

Now the modern Protestant applies this absolute idea of amputation to all parts of problematical human nature; to all popular customs or historic traditions. He does not mean that men should be restrained in them just now; he means that men should drop them for ever, like the monkey's tail. When puritans abolish ritualism, it means there shall be no more ritual. When prohibitionists abolished

---

[138] In Greek mythology, Pentheus is the Theban king murdered by the female votaries of Dionysus because he attempted to ban the worship of their god.

beer, they swore that a whole new generation would grow up and never know the taste of it. When Protestants look to the solution of Socialism, most of them do not merely mean to attack the contemporary congestion called capitalism; they mean to abolish for ever the very idea of private property.

Thus there is a fanatical quality, sweeping, final, almost suicidal, in Protestant reforms which there is *not* even in Catholic repressions. Once Puritanism pervaded America, once Prussianism pervaded Germany, there appeared a new type of law; sterilization or compulsory eugenics, from which even the dictators of the Latin tradition would shrink.

There have been any number of good Catholics who might be called puritans, from Savonarola to Manning,[139] who made their little bonfires of the vanities; but they never mistook them for the everlasting bonfire. There have been any number of bad Catholics who might be called tyrants from Borgia to Bomba,[140] who drilled or destroyed from hate or ambition; but even when torturing men they never thought they were twisting or altering Man. Therefore their prohibitions were never so prohibitionist.

Mussolini may be wrong to suppress newspapers; but who can imagine Mussolini saying, "The world will never again be cursed with printed leaves," as Jennings Bryan would say, "We shall never again be cursed with alcoholic liquor"? I think some of the recent Fascist schemes for drilling children reach the ridiculous; but they do not reach the point of saying that children should be kept from their mothers; a point which numberless Protestant progressive followers of Wells or Shaw would reach in one wild bound. In short, apart from Catholic liberty, Catholic tyranny is either temporary in the sense of a penance or a fast, or temporary in the sense of a state of siege or a proclamation of martial law. But Protestant liberty is far more oppressive than Catholic tyranny. For Protestant liberty is only

[139] Henry Edward Manning (1808–1892) was a convert to Catholicism who became archbishop of Westminster in 1865 and a cardinal ten years later.

[140] Bomba is King Ferdinand II of Naples, who earned this cognomen from his infamous bombardment of Messina in 1848.

the unlimited liberty of the rich to destroy an unlimited number of the liberties of the poor.

The B.B.C., much to the credit of its own relatively sound sense of liberty, having asked me specially for what I thought about Catholicism, I did certainly divulge the secret that I thought it was true; and that, therefore, even great cultures falling away from it, in any direction, had fallen into falsehood. I fully appreciate the desire to be fair or friendly that may lead anyone to deplore this disclosure; but I do not myself believe it will do an atom of good to anyone, least of all to the English, to whitewash or conceal the bad results of heresy in history. I was, therefore, a little puzzled when a contributor called it "a sectarian note." Somehow, I had not expected anybody on the *Catholic Herald* to call the Catholic Church a sect.

WHERE IS THE PARADOX?

A writer on a High Church paper, being full of the lyric muse, recently described me as a "prolix Papist professor of paradox"; a line which it is my firm intention to extend into a poem of no less than nine verses depending upon the letter p; by which alliterative industry the unaccountable absence of any allusion to polygamous Popes, poisoning Pontiffs, piratical prelates and pestilent peasantries, will be supplied and made good at my own expense. And though the editor very gracefully apologised for having been accidentally prevented, doubtless by my prolixity, from discovering what I actually said in the passage he criticised, another critic has since then broken out on the same paper in the same literary style; and described the same statement as going "beyond such terminological inexactitude as is permissible in the most putrid paradox"; and saying I devote myself to the propaganda of the gutter. I rather wish I knew what it is that makes the most distant prospect of me (of me, a mere dot on the crowded horizon) throw an honest gentleman at the Faith House, Tufton Street, into such astonishing convulsions. It is all the more mysterious because, so far as I am concerned, it is entirely unprovoked. I have never made any particular attack on the Anglo-Catholic theory, or the Anglican Church, or upon any Anglicans, as such. I know the Anglo-Catholic theory can be honestly held; for I held it myself for many years. I have the greatest respect for those who are in such a state of conviction; as well as the greatest sympathy for those who are in any stage of doubt. I still have a large number of Anglo-Catholic friends, who do not find me so very putrid and prolix, and, though of course I differ from them, I have always rather avoided mere dispute with them; partly because there are so many things much more in need of being disputed; and partly because I know from experience that it often does more harm than good. I used to read the paper in question because it was a good paper; and until quite recently a good-humoured paper. Why so innocuous a reader should have this extraordinary effect on the other readers and writers, I do not clearly understand. But the effect is so extraordinary that the critic falls back desperately on a sort of half-defence of Puritanism, of Protestantism and of Prussianism; though these are things which all the old Anglo-Catholics used to denounce, and which I used to denounce quite as much when I was myself an Anglo-Catholic. On a former occasion, for instance, in the same strained way, it picked a particular personal quarrel with me, merely because I joined with the whole civilised world in deploring the assassination of Dollfuss. If it were only a matter of personal quarrels, it would not be worth referring to again; for I am quite content with the admission already made about the facts in dispute; and all is gas and gaiters. But there are much more important quarrels, which concern all Christendom and especially this country, about which I can hardly leave an important organ of opinion under so false an impression.

Touching Mr. C. E. Douglas, the smeller out of putrid paradoxes, I need only record that he complains; of "an unhistorical use of the word Catholic," and assures us that we should be content with the fact that clergy of the national church are attached to nearly all our institutions, as a guarantee that "in theory, the Catholic religion is the official religion of the nation." I can only say that if he used his imagination about our point of view, as much as I try to use my imagination about his, it would, I think, dawn upon him that it is not altogether unreasonable in a real Catholic, or even a real Anglo-Catholic, to find this official reassurance a little thin. Certainly, in that sense, there are "Catholic" priests attached to all sorts of things; there is a "Catholic" bishop preaching that science has destroyed the whole original Christian scheme; there is a "Catholic" dean who booms Birth-Prevention like a quack medicine; there is a "Catholic" canon who is ready to "break bread" apparently with anybody from Mormons to Moslems; at least I myself should rather prefer the Moslems. But I cannot believe that either Mr. Douglas or the Editor of the paper really regards that retrospective breakfast as a substitute for the Blessed Sacrament. But though Mr. Douglas's view of our scruples is not highly sympathetic or discerning, there is one point on which Mr. Douglas endears himself to me, though I dare not hope that I am likely to endear myself to him. He may think what he likes about me, so long as he will go on thinking what he now thinks about Prussia. Because I classed Prussia with England among the Protestant countries, he protests against anything like a suggestion that they are the same sort of countries; and there I am warmly with him. They have certain negative things in common; but even in these it would be true to say that the Prussian prefers to be bullied where the Englishman only submits to be blinded. But England is a thousand times jollier and more human as a national culture than Prussia; the disease is milder and the mood more healthy. But it is a mood which is weakened by the absence of a militant creed of Christian morals, and the power to define and defend. The test could best be made by the introduction of some of the new abnormal laws already threatening the world in the name of science. Suppose something of the type of Compulsory Sterilisation or Compulsory Contraception really stalks through the modern State, leading the march of human progress through abortion to infanticide. If the heathens in North Germany received it, they would accept it with howls of barbaric joy, as one of the sacred commands of the Race Religion; the proceedings very probably terminating (by that time) with a little human sacrifice. If the English received it, they would accept it as law-abiding citizens; that is, as something between well-trained servants and bewildered children. There is a great difference; but not so great as the certainty that the Irish would not accept it at all.

Now the real reason why I have taken the text of these two High Church critics, is that their views happily cancel out upon a point of immense international importance. Mr. Douglas preserves his healthy instinct against Prussia, as being not improbably the source of Prussianism; though he might not admit my view that the error had its original source in Protestantism. But the other writer would protect Protestantism from any such criticism; and falls back on the jolly old catchword of calling Hitler a Catholic. Of course there are countless Catholics whom I think wrong in politics; and countless Catholics who think me wrong in politics. But I wonder if it is much truer to call Hitler a Catholic than to call Bertrand Russell an Anglo-Catholic. He was quite probably christened in an Anglican

Church. But the much more important point is the historic and cultural origin of the whole movement of the more admittedly heathenish Hitlerism. The Anglican critic says that this tribal cult of triumph began in Bavaria. It would be as sensible to say that it began in England; because it was popularised, long before anybody had ever heard of Hitler, by Houston Stewart Chamberlain.[141] In fact, the movement began before the Great War; before the Franco-Prussian War;[142] and has its origins far back in history, in the fact that the Protestant edges of Germany only partly emerged from barbarism and soon relapsed into paganism. But in its present practical form, it is simply the tail-end, we might say the rag-tag-and-bobtail of the nineteenth-century Prussianism; the camp-followers of the far better disciplined army of Bismarck. Nobody understands its very rowdy revivalism who does not understand that it is merely a revival. To suppose it began with recent headlines about Hitler is newspaper history, which is knowing no history but only news; and that frequently untrue. The movement that has actually abolished Bavaria, and left no State alive except the Bismarckian Empire, is but the last phase of the Bismarckian plan to Prussianise Germany, by crushing and outnumbering the Catholics of the Rhine; and stealing the old Imperial Crown from the other Catholics of the Danube. In short, he set up a new Protestant Empire, to dwarf and depose the old Catholic Empire; and Hitler is his heir and his executor.

These things can easily be shown to be facts, to anybody who knows anything of what happened before the newspapers of a few months ago. We need merely ask what Bavaria was like when it was Bavaria; before it felt the pressure from Prussia. When Bavaria was allowed to be Bavarian, all sorts of things were said against the Bavarians; that they were dreamy, that they were drunken, that they were ridiculously romantic, that they were mad on music, and so on. But nobody ever said that they were stiff or rigid or ruthless or inhuman or mad on mere official centralisation and militaristic discipline. That

---

[141] Houston Stewart Chamberlain (1855–1917) was an Englishman who espoused Nordic racial superiority. He moved to Germany where, after his death, his theories enjoyed popularity among the Nazis.

[142] In the Franco-Prussian War (1870–1871) France suffered a humiliating defeat.

particular sort of cold brutality came from Prussian prestige; it could not possibly have come from anything else. And that Prussianism came from Protestantism; not of course, in the sense that it came to infect all Protestants, or that there are not millions of good Protestants free from this error, or suffering from other errors. But it was a historical fruit of Protestantism; and that is not merely a historical fact; it can also be clearly traced as a philosophical truth. The racial pride of Hitlerism is of the Reformation by twenty tests; because it divides Christendom and makes all such divisions deeper; because it is fatalistic, like Calvinism, and makes superiority depend not upon choice but only on being of the chosen; because it is Caesaro-Papist, putting the State above the Church, as in the claim of Henry VIII; because it is immoral, being an innovator of morals touching things like Eugenics and Sterility; because it is subjective, in suiting the primal fact to the personal fancy, as in asking for a German God, or saying that the Catholic revelation does not suit the German temper; as if I were to say that the Solar System does not suit the Chestertonian taste. I do not apologise, therefore, for saying that this catastrophe in history has been due to heresy; and I cannot see that even an Anglo-Catholic supports his own claim to orthodoxy by denying it.

*   *   *

Naturally, I have never expected that people would agree with these views. Among the remarks which I must have spoken so badly that hardly anybody heard them, was my preliminary remark that I would very much prefer to talk to my countrymen about the things on which we should agree, about Dickens or the great comic culture of the English tradition; but that any man challenged on his allegiance to a Church must disagree with those who definitely disagree with it. I said on that occasion: "If I say these things, I cannot ask most of you to agree with me; if I did anything else, I could not ask any of you to respect me." But it does strike me, in amiable retrospect, that the whole situation is a little amusing. We live in an age in which anybody may teach anywhere, by any scientific instrument of instruction, that such a trifle as God was tossed up out of a tribal quarrel about incest or parricide, and so religion poisoned the first springs of progress; in which the Communist can claim that humanity went wrong when private property first appeared among prehistoric men; when anything, however real, in its beginning, however remote, can be called an enormous delusion darkening the whole history of man. But when I choose to think that one island, in one corner of one continent, took the wrong turning in thought at the end of one century, hardly four hundred years ago, when I attribute to that relatively recent and local fad the collapse and despair that has actually fallen on one commercial culture, a cry of protest goes up against an intolerable blasphemy; accompanied with the assurance that those who are thus horrified have, alone among all peoples, the power to tolerate all opinions.

I confess I found a faint whiff of paradox (though by no means putrid) in the fact of these few fanatics telling me in one breath that they were devoted to liberty of thought and that I had disgraced myself by saying what I thought so plainly. But they were only a few; and I ought not to close this episode without bearing testimony to the vast number of messages I received from Protestants, or even from Pagans, quite fairly recognising or quite fairly discussing, what I had really said. Above all, I know well that I could have proved my case, more clearly than appears in this hasty correspondence, if I had merely printed a correspondence far more valuable; the letters I received from very poor people, who had suffered the silent aggression and enslavement by modern monopoly; and who thanked me with only too much of the truly English generosity, for exposing the wrongs they endure with only too much of the truly English good humour.